CAREER PROGRAMMING
FOR TODAY'S TEENS

CAREER PROGRAMMING
FOR TODAY'S TEENS

Exploring Nontraditional and Vocational Alternatives

AMY WYCKOFF
MARIE HARRIS

ALA Editions

CHICAGO | 2019

AMY WYCKOFF holds a Master of Library Science from Indiana University. She currently works as a youth services senior librarian for Beaverton City Library in Beaverton, Oregon. Previously she worked for the Charlotte Mecklenburg Library in Charlotte, North Carolina, as the Loft Manager at ImaginOn. In this role, she managed a team of teen-serving librarians and library assistants. She worked with coauthor Marie Harris to plan and implement the Fast Track: Trade School Fair for its first two years. She also planned and facilitated many workforce-development and career-planning workshops for teens in the Loft. Amy worked previously for Charlotte Mecklenburg Schools as a school media specialist.

MARIE HARRIS holds a Master of Library and Information Science from the University of North Carolina at Greensboro. In 2012, she began working at the Charlotte Mecklenburg Library's Loft at ImaginOn as a teen library services specialist. While in this role, she worked with coauthor Amy Wyckoff to plan and implement the Fast Track: Trade School Fair for two years. She is currently employed as a library branch manager at the Cornelius and Davidson branches of the Charlotte Mecklenburg Library, where she manages two teams of library staff.

Extensive effort has gone into ensuring the reliability of the information in this book; however, the publisher makes no warranty, express or implied, with respect to the material contained herein.

ISBN 978-0-8389-1759-6 (paper)

Library of Congress Cataloging-in-Publication Data

Names: Wyckoff, Amy, 1982- author. | Harris, Marie, 1985- author.
Title: Career programming for today's teens : exploring nontraditional and
    vocational alternatives / Amy Wyckoff, Marie Harris.
Description: Chicago : ALA Editions, an imprint of the American Library
    Association, 2019. | Includes bibliographical references and index.
Identifiers: LCCN 2018023232 | ISBN 9780838917596 (print ; alk. paper)
Subjects: LCSH: Young adults' libraries—Activity programs. | Libraries and
    teenagers. | Vocational guidance.
Classification: LCC Z718.5 .W93 2019 | DDC 027.62/6—dc23 LC record available at https://
    lccn.loc.gov/2018023232

Cover design by Krista Joy Johnson. Images © Adobe Stock.

⊛ This paper meets the requirements of ANSI/NISO Z39.48–1992 (Permanence of Paper).

Printed in the United States of America

23 22 21 20 19   5 4 3 2 1

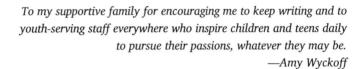

*To my supportive family for encouraging me to keep writing and to
youth-serving staff everywhere who inspire children and teens daily
to pursue their passions, whatever they may be.*
—Amy Wyckoff

*To my husband, without whom this project would have never been possible
and to my parents, who always believe in me.*
—Marie Harris

CONTENTS

PREFACE

Like so many of his peers, John is a bright and energetic teen. He is incredibly creative and talented, and not afraid of hard work. He comes into the library where we work nearly every day to use the recording sound booth. He is sure that he is going to be a star and is willing to put in the hours needed to lay down a solid track. He labors for hours over each song, adjusting the volume and balance, and rerecording parts as needed. In school, he earns decent grades in his classes. He rarely mentions his classwork to us—we get the feeling that theoretical math and classical literature simply are not important to him once he hears the final bell ring. He is a senior in high school, and we mention to him that the library is having a program about colleges and how to fill out applications. He shrugs and returns to his music. John is not alone: later, the college admittance program attracts fewer than ten attendees, and half of those are parents. There are easily twice that number of teens in the library that evening, but they show little or no interest in finding out how to write the best college applications.

John is a millennial, and he embodies many of the associated traits. He engages nearly constantly with technology throughout the day, prefers collaboration with peers over individual work, and enjoys putting his creativity to work.[1] He is eager to learn when he can see the benefits. In many cases, today's teens simply do not see the value of dedicating four more years to classwork. They are ready to jump into their careers and to contribute to society. Knowing this, it becomes easy to see why John would not be interested in learning about college applications. He might view the collegiate process as one that is highly individualized and requires long-term commitment before returning dividends. He might question this system: if he knows what he wants to do, and is motivated to learn the necessary skills, why should he also have to spend a year or two taking general education courses that are not relevant?

John and many other teens we have met during our careers have inspired us to develop creative ways to help teens as they move along the path towards whatever success looks like to them. We are inspired each day by the talent, ingenuity, and grit we see in the teens with whom we work. This book is dedicated to all teens and the library staff that devote their days to helping them. We hope this book will serve as a useful tool that will provide plenty of encouragement as you plan for programs and services for youth at your library.

NOTE

1. Debaro Huyler, Yselande Pierre, Wei Ding, and Adly Norelus, "Millennials in the Workplace: Positioning Companies for Future Success," Florida State University, http://digitalcommons.fiu.edu/cgi/viewcontent.cgi?article = 1424&context = sferc.

INTRODUCTION

Working in a bustling library located in the center of a city, we saw many teens like John. These teens were bright and energetic, but not motivated to strive towards a four-year university. We began to do some research and reading on vocational careers so that we could share that information with our teen patrons. At first, the information was shared with them in one-on-one conversations or in small group conversations. We had a regularly scheduled program in the Loft, the teen department at ImaginOn, in Charlotte, North Carolina, titled "Guy Talk." For this popular program, our male teen library services specialist would sit down with any and all guys in the Loft, share snacks, and facilitate a discussion on current issues that might affect them. Sometimes the discussion would be related to something that had been in the news recently. Other times, they would discuss options for life after high school. We began incorporating information about job-seeking and career planning, including vocational options, in Guy Talk sessions. As you've probably found in your own library, successful programs build upon themselves. We did not start off big, for example, by planning a trade school fair for 200 + participants. We started small, with a group of ten teens gathered around our teen library services specialist having a conversation about the hopes they had for their futures.

As the teens' interest in planning their futures grew, they began to ask questions of our staff outside of the formal Guy Talk sessions. We recognized their desire to learn more about the fast track to a paying career, and therefore began planning more of our programming to provide this information. Along the way, there were a few hits and misses, of course. There was a "Job Center" bulletin board where we posted written information for local job-seekers and flyers providing interview advice. Sometimes these materials were taken, but none of our teens told us that they followed through and found a job. Our teens wanted to interact directly with staff and get personalized career advice. Our one-on-one resume-building sessions were popular, as was our "Meet a Professional" series, where we invited successful professionals in vocational careers to come in and interact with our teens. Once, we had a tattoo artist present—resulting in our highest attendance for this career program series!

The Fast Track: Trade School Fair presented at ImaginOn in Charlotte, North Carolina, was the pinnacle of our journey to provide teens further opportunities to explore vocational options that went beyond one-shot resume formatting classes or college-preparatory programs. Charlotte has a robust college and university fair twice each year, but there did not seem to be any formal opportunities for teens to learn about local technical or trade schools. Our library already offered workforce-development programs to teens regularly, so we began planning the first trade school fair in the fall of 2014, to take place in the spring of 2015. Through the process of planning the event, we learned quite a bit about vocational programs in our area and about what other libraries across the nation were offering. We became excited to share that information with our teen patrons. Furthermore, we look forward to sharing information with other teen-serving library staff about library programs that support teens' interest in vocations. Later in this book, we will share detailed information about the Fast Track: Trade School Fair, and how you might replicate the program to best serve your own teen library population. We will also look at what vocational-readiness programs other libraries across the nation are already doing, or planning to do, and why these programs are essential.

WHY THE FOCUS ON TRADE SCHOOLS?

The growing "skills gap" in the United States has been documented, as we will discuss in greater detail in chapter 1. There are many employers who need employees with middle-level skills, such as those traditionally considered "the trades" or "vocations." However, there are not enough students receiving the necessary training to fill those positions. Enter the trade school (often known as vocational school). Trade schools offer fast-paced training to launch a person into a career in as little as six months to one year. These programs often limit classroom time in exchange for providing hands-on experiences. Many have training labs or arrange for their students to apprentice with local businesses. These programs allow their students to focus on the skills necessary to complete a specific job and get hired quickly. The possibility for fast results appeals to adolescents and young adults who may not have enjoyed their high school classroom experiences.

There are many reasons why vocational school would appeal to teens and young adults. Traditional four-year universities have become too costly for many students and their families. For these students, vocational programs can fast-track teens into a lucrative career, which might enable them to afford to attend a four-year university if they desire. Also, some teens need to move into their own places and start their own careers as quickly as possible after high school graduation. For these teens, a fast turnaround to a steady paycheck is a must. The programs typically run six months to two years, and the paychecks of graduates are much higher than the paychecks of students with no education beyond high school.

There are many types of vocational programs. Some of the most common include beauty and barber schools, medical and dental assistantship programs, and training for childcare workers, computer technologists, veterinary assistants, entertainment industry assistants, HVAC technicians, plumbers, and electricians. We were surprised to learn how much plumbers can earn! If more teens saw those numbers, we might have quite a few more plumbers in America. Along with private and public schools that offer vocational programs or associate's degrees, there are also numerous training centers and the Job Corps of America. The Job Corps is a program that offers housing, training, and employment to thousands of at-risk American teens each year. Graduates of the program leave with a certificate of training and essential life skills such as budgeting and time management.

PROMOTING VOCATIONAL READINESS IN YOUR LIBRARY

How can we teen librarians support and encourage teens pursuing these opportunities? What kinds of programs can we offer to help prepare teens for these opportunities? In this book, we'll see examples from libraries across the country: everything from in-library internships to drop-in resume-building programs to major career or vocational school fairs. We will give advice on planning programs to fit your library, budget, and teen population. Further, we will share success stories about building partnerships with other youth-serving organizations in your community.

Chapter 1 focuses on the research on trade school trends. Trade schools and certificate programs for teens and young adults are becoming more common, and the outlook indicates that their popularity will only continue to grow.

Chapter 2 covers career-focused programming in libraries. We will look at the reasons why this type of programming can be a good fit in your library, and explore successful programs already taking place in libraries across the nation.

Chapter 3 presents ideas for getting teens interested in and excited about career-focused programming at the library. We include examples of successful incentives that a variety of libraries have used to help attract teens.

Chapter 4 outlines the components of ImaginOn's "Meet a Professional" program series. We will present ideas about which careers to target and share stories of success from our most popular career representatives.

Chapter 5 examines a variety of internship models within public libraries and their benefits for teens and for the libraries that host them. These programs provide teens with real-world work experience within a library setting and are often administered by the Teen Services staff member.

Chapter 6 details ImaginOn's annual Fast Track: Trade School Fair. We have shared our planning time line, a list of possible vocational training programs to contact, and how to execute a successful event, should you wish to replicate this one.

Chapter 7 highlights actual vocational or certificate training programs offered within library settings, such as presenter-offered classes, and explores how to facilitate MOOCs and Learning Circles by providing space in which teens can participate. Beyond simply informing patrons about potential opportunities external to the library, these programs conclude with the participant receiving a certificate of skills acquired.

Chapter 8 covers options for partnering with your local schools and other organizations to further your career-readiness programming capabilities. Many high schools have begun offering vocational training or vocational training information, and the library can support and further those programs.

Chapter 9 examines program assessment. We will discuss how to determine your teen patrons' needs and desires, and how to evaluate the effectiveness of your career-readiness programs.

Chapter 10 provides collection development advice related to career planning for teens. We have highlighted current titles to consider adding to your collection, as well as selection tools for building a professional resource collection.

Over the last three years, we have been continually inspired by our teens' reactions to information about vocations. They love hearing that there are programs available that will fast-track them to careers and that there are so many options for possible careers. We are excited to share information that we have learned about these programs and to help you get started energizing your own teen patrons.

Trade School Trends

SCHOOL ADMINISTRATORS OFTEN TALK ABOUT ensuring that students are college– and career–ready when they graduate from high school. This is no easy task for high school administrators and teachers to accomplish. A push towards ensuring that America's youth are career-ready was a focus of President Barack Obama's presidency. During his 2013 State of the Union address, he called on America's high schools to redesign their educational programs to better prepare students for life beyond graduation: "I'm announcing a new challenge to redesign America's high schools so they better equip graduates for the demands of a high-tech economy. We'll reward schools that develop new partnerships with colleges and employers, and create classes that focus on science, technology, engineering, and math—the skills today's employers are looking for to fill jobs right now and in the future."[1]

Many school systems have accepted President Obama's challenge by developing and implementing new programs by partnering with companies or community colleges. Many school administrators are seeking unique ways to bring real-life job-skills training into their high schools as a way of better preparing students for the opportunities of the future. What might these newly designed high school curricula look like? The US Department of Education lists the following Principles of Next Generation High Schools:

- redesigning academic content and instructional practices to promote active and hands-on learning aligned with postsecondary and career-readiness;
- personalizing and tailoring academic content and learning to strengthen the connection to the educational needs and interests of individual students;
- ensuring strong content knowledge and skills for teachers in all subjects, including STEM;
- providing and personalizing academic and wrap-around support services for those students who need them;
- providing high-quality career and college exploration and counseling on options for students after high school graduation;
- offering multiple opportunities to engage in postsecondary learning, including earning college credit while still in high school; and
- redesigning the scope and sequence of learning time in more innovative and meaningful ways, incorporating innovations such as educational technologies, project-based learning, and competency-based progressions.[2]

This focus on the importance of teens acquiring the skills they will need to be successful adults is not new; however, a focus on the rising costs of four-year college programs, especially at private institutions, has been a frequent topic in the media recently. During the 2016 presidential election, the rising cost of college education and the prevalence of debt accumulated after four years of tuition payments was a topic discussed during several debates. It is now estimated that there is over $1 trillion in student loan debt, which exceeds the amount of credit card debt held by Americans.[3] Students who wish to avoid many years of student loan payments are seeking other options for their education, including pathways to many lucrative careers in the areas that have traditionally been called "the trades." Becoming skilled in these trades often requires a six-month to two-year certificate or degree. These careers will be covered in greater depth later in this chapter.

TREND TOWARDS VOCATIONAL CAREERS

There is a great need for individuals who can fill middle-skill careers—jobs that require more than a high school diploma, but less than a four-year degree. What is most often needed to fill these middle-skill level jobs is people with specialized training and skills that can be acquired from an associate's degree program or certificate program. Employers are facing a "skills gap," which means they cannot fill positions because there are not enough applicants who have the necessary skills.[4]

According to the National Skills Coalition, a nonprofit working toward a vision of an America that grows its economy by investing in workers, more than half (approximately 54 percent) of all jobs in the United States fall into this middle-skill category. Its findings show that only 44 percent of Americans currently have the training required to be eligible for these positions. Millions of other Americans could be qualified for these positions if they were able to acquire the education needed. However, for people who do not have access to such educational programs, these jobs remain unattainable.[5]

Some large employers, such as John Deere, are working directly with community colleges to ensure that curriculum will enable students to acquire the necessary skills to be ready for their future careers. The number of middle-skill-level jobs will continue to increase in the future, according to data from the US Department of Labor, which means students graduating from programs that have prepared them to step into these career fields will find they have gainful employment readily available to them. Figure 1.1. shows data collected in 2016 by the US Bureau of Labor Statistics that illustrates the fastest growing occupations and their median salaries. The figure also shows the rate at which these career fields are expected to grow from 2016 through 2026.

A trend towards STEM education and a hands-on learning environment in many high schools is helping prepare students to be ready for programs in many of the STEM-based careers listed in figure 1.1. These jobs will be in high demand when today's high school students graduate and achieve any subsequent degrees they pursue. Many students will find a career in the fields listed in figure 1.1 to be not only rewarding, but also financially lucrative.

FIGURE 1.1

Fastest growing occupations in 2016 and projected 2026 (numbers in thousands)

2016 National Employment Matrix title and code	Employment		Change, 2016-26		Median annual wage, 2016*
	2016	2026	Number	Percent	
Total, all occupations	156,063.8	167,582.3	11,518.6	7.4	$37,040
Solar photovoltaic installers	11.3	23.1	11.8	104.9	$39,240
Wind turbine service technicians	5.8	11.3	5.6	96.3	$52,260
Home health aides	911.5	1,342.7	431.2	47.3	$22,600
Personal care aides	2,016.1	2,793.8	777.6	38.6	$21,920
Physician assistants	106.2	145.9	39.6	37.3	$101,480
Nurse practitioners	155.5	211.6	56.1	36.1	$100,910
Statisticians	37.2	49.8	12.6	33.8	$80,500
Physical therapist assistants	88.3	115.8	27.4	31.0	$56,610
Software developers, applications	831.3	1,086.6	255.4	30.7	$100,080
Mathematicians	3.1	4.0	0.9	29.7	$105,810
Physical therapist aides	52.0	67.2	15.3	29.4	$25,680
Bicycle repairers	12.4	16.1	3.6	29.3	$27,630
Medical assistants	634.4	818.4	183.9	29.0	$31,540
Genetic counselors	3.1	4.0	0.9	29.0	$74,120
Occupational therapy assistants	39.3	50.7	11.4	28.9	$59,010

FIGURE 1.1 (CONTINUED)

2016 National Employment Matrix title and code	Employment		Change, 2016-26		Median annual wage, 2016*
	2016	2026	Number	Percent	
Information security analysts	100.0	128.5	28.5	28.5	$92,600
Physical therapists	239.8	306.9	67.1	28.0	$85,400
Operations research analysts	114.0	145.3	31.3	27.4	$79,200
Forest fire inspectors and prevention specialists	1.7	2.2	0.5	26.6	$36,230
Massage therapists	160.3	202.4	42.1	26.3	$39,860
Health specialties teachers, postsecondary	233.5	294.0	60.6	25.9	$99,360
Derrick operators, oil and gas	11.1	13.9	2.8	25.7	$48,130
Roustabouts, oil and gas	50.0	62.4	12.4	24.8	$37,340
Occupational therapy aides	7.5	9.3	1.8	24.7	$28,330
Phlebotomists	122.7	152.8	30.1	24.5	$32,710
Nonfarm animal caretakers	241.5	300.0	58.5	24.2	$21,990
Rotary drill operators, oil and gas	16.7	20.8	4.0	24.2	$54,430
Nursing instructors and teachers, postsecondary	67.9	84.2	16.3	24.0	$69,130
Occupational therapists	130.4	161.4	31.0	23.8	$81,910
Service unit operators, oil, gas, and mining	41.4	51.1	9.7	23.4	$48,610

*Data are from the Occupational Employment Statistics program, U.S. Bureau of Labor Statistics. Wage data cover non-farm wage and salary workers and do not cover the self-employed, owners, and partners in unincorporated firms, or household workers.

Source: Employment Projections program, U.S. Bureau of Labor Statistics. April 14, 2017. www.bls.gov/emp/ep_table_103.htm.

WHAT CERTIFICATE PROGRAMS ARE AVAILABLE?

When people think of trade school programs, often cosmetology is one of the first programs to come to mind. This is a great option, of course, but there are many other programs to consider. Certificate programs range from medical technology to computer engineering and construction management. A list of popular vocational programs follows.

- nursing
- veterinary technology
- radiology
- automotive mechanics
- welding
- audio engineering and sound recording
- business management
- massage therapy
- landscape design
- culinary arts
- restaurant management

- hospitality
- plumbing
- bioscience technology
- accounting
- civil engineering
- administrative assistantship
- machine manufacturing
- video production
- paralegal studies
- property management
- video game design
- dental hygiene

These programs are designed to be completed in six months to two years on average so that students can quickly apply their newly earned degrees towards successful careers. The list of popular programs is by no means exhaustive; however, it does provide a quick look at the range of programs available to students looking for a next step after high school.

EARNING POTENTIAL OF CAREERS THAT DO NOT REQUIRE A FOUR-YEAR DEGREE

There is a common misconception that careers only requiring an associate's degree, a certificate, or on-the-job training are likely to pay far less than careers requiring four-year or graduate degrees. However, we find this is not the case if we examine the earning potential of some of the common careers that do not require a bachelor's degree. Figure 1.2 features data from *Peterson's College Quest* that shows the top twenty-five highest paying jobs that only require an associate's degree as well as the projected growth for these fields.[6]

FIGURE 1.2
Top 25 highest paying jobs that require only an Associate's degree

Profession	Medium Annual Income	Projected Growth
Air Traffic Controllers	$121,280	Little or no change expected by 2022
Radiation Therapist	$79,140	Expected to grow at a much faster than average rate of 24% by 2022
Nuclear Technicians	$72,610	Projected to grow 15% by 2022
Nuclear Medicine Technologists	$71,120	Projected to grow 20% by 2022
Dental Hygienists	$71,110	Expected to grow at a much faster than average rate of 33% by 2022
Funeral Service Managers	$68,420	Projected to grow 12% by 2022
Diagnostic Medical Sonographers (1) and Cardiovascular Technologists and Technicians (2)	$66,410 (1) $53,210 (2)	Expected to grow at a much faster than average rate of 46% (1); 30% (2)
Registered Nurses	$66,220	Expected to grow at a much faster than average rate of 19% by 2022
Web Developers	$63,160	Expected to grow at a much faster than average rate of 20% by 2022
Aerospace Engineering and Operations Technicians	$62,680	Little or no change expected by 2022
Computer Network Support Specialists	$60,180	Projected to grow 7% by 2022
Electrical and Electronics Engineering Technicians	$58,540	Little or no change expected by 2022

(cont.)

FIGURE 1.2 (CONTINUED)

Respiratory Therapists	$56,290	Expected to grow at a much faster than average rate of 19% by 2022
Aircraft and Avionics Equipment Mechanics (1) and Technicians (2)	$55,980 (1) $55,990 (2)	Little or no change expected by 2022
Radiologic (1) and MRI Technicians (2)	$55,500 (1) $66,050 (2)	Expected to grow at a much faster than average rate of 21% by 2022
Geological and Petroleum Technicians	$53,410	Projected to grow 15% by 2022
Mechanical Engineering Technicians	$52,390	Projected to grow 5% by 2022
Electro-mechanical Technicians	$51,330	Projected to grow 4% by 2022
Industrial Engineering Technicians	$52,020	Projected to decline by 3% by 2022
Drafters	$49,630	Little or no change expected by 2022
Civil Engineering Technicians	$47,570	Little or no change expected by 2022
Paralegals and Legal Assistants	$47,570	Projected to grow 17% by 2022
Environmental Engineering Technicians	$46,160	Projected to grow 18% by 2022
Medical Equipment Repairers	$44,180	Expected to grow at a much faster than average rate of 30% by 2022
Chemical Technicians	$43,310	Projected to grow 9% by 2022

There are many careers for people without four-year degrees that pay well above the national average salary. Many of the careers attainable with an associate's degree that have the highest earning potentials are STEM-related, either in the fields of computer technology or medicine. If students are interested in a STEM field as a career, they have many options available for programs that will lead to success. In addition to earning potential, individuals in these challenging career fields often report high job satisfaction and motivation to advance in their fields.

Choosing a career that does not require a four-year degree also allows individuals to start earning a good salary sooner, and therefore pay off any debt they may have acquired while pursuing their degree or certificate. If students attend a community college for their degree or certificate, they are likely to have acquired minimal debt, which means they can start saving more quickly.

REASONS TEENS ARE CHOOSING VOCATIONAL PROGRAMS

Over the years, we have met many teens who were not interested in attending a four-year college. There could be several reasons for their disinterest in attending a four-year college or university, including:

- no one else in their family has attended college and the family does not discuss this as an option for the future
- their families cannot afford to send them to college and they are unaware of scholarships or think they would not qualify for them
- their families are relying on them to help at home, financially or otherwise, and they cannot spare the time to attend classes or go away to school
- they have dropped out of high school and no longer consider college to be an option
- they prefer to participate in online programs rather than attending classes in person
- they disliked high school and do not wish to pursue further schooling

For each of the reasons above, a six-month to two-year degree or certificate program might be the perfect option. Often these programs are completed close to home. Because the programs may be part-time, students can work while completing the requirements. Community colleges offer affordable programs and often have counselors who can advise students about the options for federal student aid.

Online degrees may be preferred by some students for a variety of reasons. Associate's degree programs and certificate programs are widely available online. Students should also be mindful that although many online degree programs offered by for-profit institutions may have a high price tag, there are many lower-cost online programs offered by community college institutions as well or partial online and in-person programs.

What about those students who truly disliked high school and are not looking forward to attending school again? We have all met teens who cringe at the word *school* or *college*. We have seen these same teens come alive in programs when they are given the chance to perform a song, solve a problem, or design a video game. Trade schools provide an opportunity for individuals to dive deep into their passions and capitalize on their strengths. Of course, there will be challenging classes with tough exams, but vocational programs generally engage students in more real-life and hands-on training than high schools. Four-year colleges often require students to complete approximately one year's worth of courses in general education (e.g., math, writing, public speaking, science, and often a foreign language), which may set some students up for failure. We have met many students who dropped out of four-year universities, but then were highly successful in two-year or certificate programs. Some of these students reported feeling more focused as students in an associate's degree program because they could visualize their end goal more concretely and stay more focused throughout the program.

VOCATIONAL PROGRAMS IN US SCHOOLS

Across the country, there are newly introduced programs connecting students with college courses or vocational training within their own high school classrooms. These programs are in direct response to the idea that our current educational standards are not preparing students to make a successful transition from high school to gainful employment.

Dual-enrollment programs in US high schools are making it even easier for students to secure job training before graduating from high school. These programs may be called things like "early college" or "middle college" to designate that the students enrolled are still in high school. A number of California high schools now allow students to complete two years of college credits while attending high school—this means they graduate with a high school diploma and an associate's degree at the same time.[7] In addition, students in dual-enrollment programs receive the added benefit of being more likely to graduate high school.[8] Dual-enrollment programs already exist in many areas of the country and additional programs are being established as more families realize the abundant benefits of the programs.

The National Alliance of Concurrent Enrollment Partnerships (NACEP) helps ensure that the classes being offered as part of dual-enrollment programs at high schools are as rigorous as the same courses that are offered on the partner college's campus so that students earning these college credits are being challenged academically at a college level. NACEP also collects and shares data about the health of dual-enrollment programs across the country. According to NACEP, students in four out of five high schools take college courses while still enrolled in high school. Many of these students take college courses within the walls of their own high schools. They may be taught by a high school teacher who has received accreditation from the college to teach the college-level material or instructors from the college campus may visit the school to teach classes. Most of the students enrolled in these programs are high school juniors and seniors who are preparing for lives after high school.[9]

There are a number of companies that have created partner programs with local high schools or community colleges as a way to help define an educational path for students interested in a career in a specific field. When Siemens determined there was a need to fill jobs at their Charlotte, North Carolina, factory, and that there were not enough local skilled applicants, it created an apprenticeship program in 2011 for seniors at local high schools. The program combines four years of job training with an associate's degree in mechatronics from nearby Central Piedmont Community College. Because of the program, students graduate with no student loan debt and can start earning $50,000 right after they complete the program.[10]

THE DIMINISHING STIGMA OF TRADES

For many years, underachievers and students considered unable to complete college-level work were pushed into vocational programs in US high schools. We have all likely viewed movies where the troublemakers were enrolled in shop class or automotive repair rather than English or advanced math classes. As a result, many people view the vocations in a negative light. However, many of these vocational fields require an advanced level of skill and problem-solving ability. As we saw earlier, these vocational trades often pay salaries above the national average and are likely to see job growth over the next decade.

Apprenticeships and internships are making a strong comeback. They offer students job training without debt and often an immediate job opportunity after completion. President Obama's administration allocated $265 million for apprenticeship programs, and his secretary of labor, Thomas E. Perez, focused on rebranding these programs so they would have a greater appeal for teachers, students, and their families. He encouraged community colleges and companies to establish partnerships that would provide on-the-job training that grant academic credit towards degrees.[11]

STEM careers are helping to highlight the country's trend toward innovation, creation, and design. As figure 1.1 illustrates, there will continue to be growth in these career fields, and students with technological skills will be poised to fill open positions.

CONCLUSION

The demand for applicants who can fill middle-skill level jobs continues to increase. Teens and young adults who are able to learn the necessary skills will find there are many employment opportunities available for them. Dual-enrollment programs in high schools across the United States allow teens to acquire college credits at no charge while also completing their high school diplomas. These programs have been shown to be rigorous, ensuring teens can successfully acquire the skills needed to enter the workforce right after high school, or be prepared to enroll in another college-level program after graduation. These programs are helping to break down the stereotype that vocational education is meant for those teens who are not prepared for college-level academics. Many vocational programs require a high level of skills and problem-solving.

The remainder of this book will focus on some of the efforts we can make as library staff to illustrate the types of vocational programs and careers available to teens and to help them discover resources about careers related to their interests.

Notes

1. "Transcript: Obama's State of the Union Address as Prepared for Delivery," February 12, 2013, www.npr.org/2013/02/12/171841852/transcript-obamas-state-of -the-union-as-prepared-for-delivery.
2. US Department of Education, "Next Generation High Schools: Redesigning the American High School Experience," May 6, 2017, www.ed.gov/next-generation -high-schools.
3. Jenna Goudreau, "The Ten Best-Paying Jobs for Community College Grads," *Forbes*, December 18, 2012, www.forbes.com/sites/jennagoudreau/2012/12/18/ the-10-best-paying-jobs-for-community-college-grads/#25d972c175db.
4. Jeffrey J. Selingo, "Wanted: Factory Workers, Degree Required," *The New York Times,* January 30, 2017, https://www.nytimes.com/2017/01/30/education/ edlife/factory-workers-college-degree-apprenticeships.html.

5. National Skills Coalition, "Adult Education: A Crucial Foundation for Middle-Skill Jobs," May 1, 2017, www.nationalskillscoalition.org/resources/publications/file/9.26-NSC-AdultEd-factsheet_final.pdf.

6. "The 25 Top High Paying Jobs with an Associate's Degree," *Peterson's College Quest*, April 25, 2017, http://www.collegequest.com/top-high-paying-jobs-with-an-associates-degree.aspx.

7. California Department of Education, "Dual and Concurrent Enrollment Strategies," January 5, 2017, www.cde.ca.gov/ci/gs/hs/duenconstgs.asp.

8. Melinda Mechur Karp, Juan Carlos Calcagno, Katherine L. Hughes, Dong Wook Jeong, and Thomas Bailey, "The Postsecondary Achievement of Participants in Dual Enrollment: An Analysis of Student Outcomes in Two States, Community College Research Center, February 2008, https://ccrc.tc.columbia.edu/media/k2/attachments/dual-enrollment-student-outcomes-brief.pdf.

9. National Alliance of Concurrent Enrollment Partnerships, May 1, 2017, www.nacep.org.

10. Selingo, "Wanted: Factory Workers."

11. Ibid.

Career Programming
at the Library

TEENS ENTER HIGH SCHOOL AND SPEND THE NEXT four years taking general education classes and maybe some Advanced Placement (AP) classes, enjoying elective arts classes, and playing sports or music. Maybe in their senior year it will occur to some of them to begin applying to colleges. Often, their college choices are based more on their favorite sports team or where the school is located than on the school's academic rating and programs of study offered.

Even in their senior year of high school, teens are expected to raise their hands and ask permission to leave the classroom to use the restroom. Their teachers give them daily reminders of homework assignments that are due. Often, their parents are still their chauffeurs, ensuring that they safely arrive on time for their various activities. Then, during the three months between graduating from high school and beginning college, they are expected to grow up enough to know what they should major in, what their future career will be, and how to achieve that goal without the constant aid of parents and teachers.

One of the main activities of guidance counselors in high schools is to help students prepare for life after high school. These professionals are meant to be available to students to help them explore and discuss different career options and discover the corresponding programs of study that they would need to pursue after high school. Guidance counselors should instruct students on time-management and planning skills. They should be able to help students define their career paths and find training or certificate programs, colleges, or universities that would help them attain their goals. A counselor should be a great resource for high school students.

However, there is a shocking shortage of guidance counselors in public high schools in the United States. Although the American School Counselor Association recommends a ratio no greater than 250 students to each counselor (which sounds too high to us), most schools have student-counselor ratios well above that. In Arizona, the average school guidance counselor is responsible for more than 900 students! The national average is 491 students to each counselor.[1] Although a guidance counselor should be helping advise students on many aspects of life during and after high school, many can barely keep up with nearly 500 students' schedule change requests and transcripts. When a counselor could be helping Bobby figure out if a vocational school or four-year university is a better fit for him, the counselor is instead helping fill out the paperwork for Susy to switch from AP Math to AP Biology. From our experience in public schools in Charlotte, North Carolina, we also know that guidance counselors are often called on to assist students who are involved in crisis situations, either inside the school walls or in their lives outside of the school. They are often called on to resolve verbal or physical disputes among students and then to meet with these students to help them avoid fights in the future. These are undoubtedly important responsibilities for the counselors, but it can be time-consuming to help students in crisis. This means counselors have limited time to meet with students to discuss their career goals.

We have talked with a few students who attend a large public high school in Charlotte, North Carolina, about how often they met with their guidance counselors. They all reported that they sometimes saw their counselors in the hallways and at lunch, but that they did not have formal meetings with them unless a student or parent requested one. They noted that they sometimes asked to meet with their counselor if there were issues with their schedules, but the meetings were often very brief and rushed, especially at the beginning of the semester when the counselor was dealing with many other schedule change requests. Sometimes a schedule request was handled by e-mail between the counselor and the parent and an in-person meeting was not even necessary. Students at large schools had very little face-time with their counselors, and most did not feel their counselors knew them or their goals personally. We are not in any way implying that guidance counselors at public schools are inadequate or unskilled; rather, these professionals are often highly skilled, but may have too much on their plates to be able to serve the whole student body. A school with multiple full-time counselors would be in a better place to serve students' needs.

It is quite rare for a public high school to offer career guidance or exploration as a class. In the few instances where it is offered, it is either explicitly or implicitly directed to Special Education/Exceptional Child students. Classes on professional dress and business communication, resume building, job-seeking, and potential avenues for training or certification may serve students with special needs well, but it is a shame that so many other students miss the opportunity to benefit from these classes. We often offer these types of programs at the public library, and students and their parents report that this is the first time the students have had the opportunity to learn about some of these important job training skills. As our public schools continue to fall behind in funding for programs, career exploration classes, along with Home Economics and Shop, will only get cut more and more often. Without classes that instruct students on what to expect after high school, how can we expect them to make smart choices?

VOCATIONAL PROGRAMMING AND DROPOUT RATES

Teens are more likely to be engaged in high school when they can clearly see the relevance of their studies to a future goal. Vocational programs within high schools have been shown to have "positive effects on students' degree attainment (college), college access and enrollment, credit accumulation, completing high school, and general academic achievement (high school)."[2] Dual-enrollment programs, sometimes referred to as early college programs, began to become popular in the 1990s and have continued to gain popularity in many places across the United States. When teachers and administrators see that students in these programs thrive, graduate high school, and move on to lucrative careers or college, they become advocates of these programs and want to see more students take advantage of this opportunity.

We became aware of this type of program because the community college in Charlotte, North Carolina, offers what it calls a Middle College program. Central Piedmont's Career and College Promise program allows students enrolled in Charlotte Mecklenburg Schools to enroll in dual-enrollment courses free of charge.[3] We would often see teens in the library during school hours, and upon discussion with them, we would learn that they were part of the program. Most of these students reported they enjoyed the chance to take college classes and to be on an actual college campus while their peers were in high school classes. The Middle College requires that they develop time-management skills and be responsible for getting themselves to classes on campus on time by car or by bus. In other words, they were practicing skills to be successful in high school, college, and in their future careers of choice.

Importantly, dual-enrollment programs offered to high school students can help close the achievement gap and provide additional scaffolding to help all students succeed. Recent research "shows that early college high schools are a particularly effective approach to improving college access and completion for low-income students and students of color."[4] We have often heard school administrators and politicians exclaim that we must do all we can to close this achievement gap, but it remains. In fact, "less than 10 percent of children born in the bottom quartile of household incomes attain a bachelor's degree by age twenty-five, compared to over 50 percent in the top quartile. Many high school students—especially those from low-income backgrounds—lack access to the rigorous coursework and support services that help prepare them for success in college."[5]

Many students who graduate high school are surprised to find that their college deems them to not be college-ready; unfortunately, remedial classes have been found to be a major cause contributing to America's record rate of college dropout. Early college programs have a curriculum designed to prepare students for college-level work so that they do not have to enroll in remedial classes at the start of the college experience. This also makes sense in terms of financial savings, because the "additional cost to run an early college program, pegged at about $700 to $900 per student per year, is substantially less than what colleges spend on remediation—to say nothing of the earnings lost and the debt incurred when students leave college with no degree."[6] The financial costs when students arrive at college unprepared for college-level work are shared by the student and the financial institution.

Students arriving at college are more likely to drop out if they face a semester or two of remedial courses. According to research by the National Council of State Legislatures, students required to complete remedial courses take longer to obtain their degrees; in some cases, these classes have been found to delay—and for some, ultimately prevent—them from attaining a college degree.[7] There is a demographic gap in the need for remediation: "56 percent of African American students and 45 percent of Latino students enroll in remedial courses nationwide, compared with 35 percent of white students."[8] Since low-income Hispanic and African American students are more often required to complete remedial courses than peers who are white or from wealthier backgrounds, students from more advantaged backgrounds will be less likely to be tripped up by remedial coursework. These remedial classes penalize those students who have already been determined to lag measurably behind their peers in terms of scores in certain subjects. Yet colleges and universities continue to require remedial coursework for incoming students who have fallen behind their peers.

Students in dual-enrollment programs will be more likely to graduate high school and, should they choose to pursue college, are more likely to be college-ready. Dual-enrollment programs help schools "catch weaknesses early, which can help a student avoid costly and time-consuming remedial classes later."[9] If students are made aware of how they can improve their grades, they can catch up and avoid being required to enroll in remedial math and English classes during their first semester of college. This can be an embarrassing and costly surprise to incoming college freshman, especially when the issue could have been identified for them earlier had the right structure been in place.

Dual-enrollment programs by nature have a future-facing structure. Instructors may help students construct goals for their futures and serve as guidance counselors without the designated title. For students who may have little opportunity for interaction with the guidance counselors at their schools, this might make all the difference in their lives beyond high school. For example, consider a dual-enrollment program that focuses on engineering such as the Pre-Engineering Certification Pathway, a partnership between the Louisiana Board of Elementary and Secondary Education and Louisiana State University. In addition to the engineering coursework these high school students will complete, they will also be exposed to "a firsthand understanding of engineering as a profession." As the Associate Dean of Academic Affairs at the LSU College of Engineering explains, "high school students do not understand where an engineering profession could lead them and are unfamiliar with the various engineering fields."[10] This program will allow them to explore this field well beyond what they would encounter during a more general high school education.

To illustrate the focus early colleges place on helping students succeed beyond high school, here's a job posting for an Early College Liaison (Academic Program Specialist) posted on May 26, 2017:

The Early College Liaison serves as an intermediary between Hostos Community College and HERO High School, with the mission of strengthening student performance and expanding students' horizons to include postsecondary educational opportunities and career goals. Through this partnership, the students are able to earn college credits toward their associate degree while earning a high school diploma. As part of this educational experience, the liaison works with the college faculty and staff to develop non-credit bearing programs and events to support this goal. Working together with the college and school personnel, the liaison seeks to maintain and develop collaborations that serve to better prepare students for college and careers while fostering mutual learning among the faculty, staff, and students at the partnering institutions. The liaison is instrumental in facilitating students' progress and success by ensuring that appropriate collaborative support mechanisms are in place, so it is highly recommended that this person have experience working with both high school students and adults (i.e. professors, teachers, parents, and school leadership). The ability to develop strong working relationships needs to be combined with strong organizational skills around the various administrative responsibilities.

Reporting to the Director of School-College Partnerships, the successful candidate will perform the following duties in addition to those in the overview:

- Serves as a liaison between Hostos Community College and HERO High School in all areas of communication and logistics.
- Monitors student progress in pre-college and college classes, including ongoing communication with students, school leaders, professors, and high school instructors.
- Coordinates student academic support services for students in college courses including tutoring.
- Convenes and participates in regular planning meetings with college and school staff that focuses primarily on the ongoing development of the scope and sequence of the school, the development

of early college partnership activities and curriculum development.

• Manages the admissions and enrollment processes for college courses; communicates with professors and high school instructors to monitor progress.

• Assists the school in monitoring and evaluating program data, as well as data from the city and state examinations, to assess student progress and to make recommendations to improve student achievement in order to fulfill the early college mission.[11]

Note the depth of involvement expected of the professional in this position. This person will be expected to monitor student progress and coordinate academic support, including tutoring. Students enrolled in these programs often receive additional services to help them create goals, plan for their futures, and take the steps needed to succeed. This additional resource can make the difference in whether they drop out of high school or college, especially if they lack academic support in their home lives.

Raven Osborne attended GEO Foundation's 21st Century Charter School in Gary, Indiana, and earned a college degree two weeks before graduating with her high school diploma. "'It was definitely a lot of work," she says, adding that to help her stay motivated, her mom, "did remind me that the goal wasn't too far off, and I was near the finish line. And . . . I had support from GEO, I had support from some people at 21st Century, so I was surrounded by support.'"[12] More support from teachers and administrators and keeping an eye on future goals help students in dual-enrollment programs stay focused on their work and achieve success.

HOW DO TEENS SELECT A CAREER?

Our research and our discussions with high school students have led us to the unfortunate conclusion that many students are not receiving career guidance as part of their high school education. In their high school years, many students have abandoned their childhood daydreams of becoming veterinarians, firefighters, or professional athletes. So where does that leave high school students on the brink of beginning their adult lives? How do they transition from being teenagers and full-time students to a "career"? Some students may find this stressful and intimidating. Other students may be excited about their future plans. What we have often found is that teenagers are likely not giving much thought to life beyond high school and how they will be able to jump-start a career in a field that they will enjoy.

Media sources that teens read, watch, or listen to can have a strong influence on how teens view certain types of careers. When we asked teens about their favorite television shows, they named those that featured older teens. We realized many of the characters are teens on the brink of adulthood, with the big question of "what will my career be?" looming on the horizon. For example, many teens mentioned the show *Blackish's* character Zoey, who visited college campuses in 2017, trying to determine her future career path. Our favorite shows as teenagers also featured characters struggling with ideas about their future lives and careers. Magazines marketed to teens often feature articles with tips about selecting a career field or about teens who discovered some passion or strength that led them to pursue an impressive career like fashion or app development.

Teen magazines and their websites float clever ways to help teens quell their anxiety about choosing a career or first choosing a college to attend. Why not select a college that best corresponds to your astrological sign?

> Need some inspiration as you start choosing which colleges to apply to? Your sign can show you the way! Whether you're a social butterfly Libra who needs a big school with lots of entertainment and student activities or an Aquarius who would fit in better with a more intimate type of school that allows for more one-on-one interaction, there's a campus out there for your personality. Find your sign below to see what type of school is best for you, according to the zodiac.[13]

With so many different influences on teens, we wanted to learn more from them about how they go about selecting a career and how they would get started on their goals.

A TEEN'S PERSPECTIVE ON SELECTING A CAREER

When Amy first moved to Portland, she spent some time as a substitute teacher. This turned out to be a serendipitous experience that helped with writing this book. A perfect chance to ask teens about future career planning, right? She wanted to learn how much time they were spending considering their future careers and what resources they were using to make these decisions. She found that some students were all too excited to share their future goals and others did not want to entertain her question for long. Overall, there were more students who fell into the latter group—students who were not really thinking too much about future careers or the steps they would need to take to achieve a future career goal.

While pursuing a high school diploma, how many opportunities do students have in the classroom to explore career options and discuss which field might be a good fit? The scarcity of guidance counselors and the lack of career exploration coursework in most American high schools has already been discussed. Do students talk to parents or other trusted adults in their lives? Are they too busy with activities or distracted by the noise of high school drama and social media to think about their futures?

To discover the answers to these questions, several for-profit and nonprofit organizations attempt to engage students about the issue. Internships and counseling can help students consider options for the future. For example, in Charlotte, North Carolina, The Relatives, a system of resources for youth, operate a facility called On Ramp that is a "Resource Center for any young adult 16–24 years old in Mecklenburg County who may need help making the successful evolution from youth to being an independent adult."[14] While working at ImaginOn, which was only a few blocks from On Ramp, Amy met many teens who reported that counselors at On Ramp were not only helping them to find a jobs so they could make money in the present day, but also helping them to explore the next step for their lives—whether that was more education or preparing for a better-paying job that might offer a higher level of job satisfaction.

Job satisfaction was a topic that came up often when Amy spoke to high school students about a future career—although they did not use the phrase "job satisfaction." They talked about not wanting a "boring" job or one that required them to "sit in an office all day." They wanted a job that they "liked" and did not "hate going to each day." Some teens mentioned these things but then did not know exactly what that career would be. This is like Lloyd Dobler in the movie *Say Anything:* "A career? I've thought about this quite a bit, sir, and I would have to say considering what's waiting out there for me, I don't want to sell anything, buy anything or process anything as a career. I don't want to sell anything bought or processed or buy anything sold or processed or repair anything sold, bought or processed as a career."[15]

Right on the front page of the Find Your Calling website, which was developed for an audience of teens, young adults, and their parents, the following statistics are presented in bold:

- 70 percent of college students graduate in debt. The average is $35,000.
- 87 percent are bored at work.
- 47 percent of college grads can't find a job related to their education.
- 500,000 workers missed their calling. They wish they had picked a different major.[16]

Unfortunately, selecting a career that will be both enjoyable and lucrative is not as simple as completing an online questionnaire. This major life decision takes much thought and a variety of life experiences. We asked a group of teens "how do you know which career to choose if you aren't sure about all the options available as careers?" Their responses follow:

John: My parents try to talk to me about careers in science and technology because I like games and have good grades in math. They said I should be looking into programs at schools that offer careers I might like—like tech schools. They said if I keep my grades up in math and science and also my other classes, I might get scholarships. They said I can think about the job I would want while at college because I can learn more about the options from my classes there.

Isa: My mom cleans houses and she doesn't want me to do that. She's had to do lots of jobs to take care of my sister and me. She wants me to go to college and get a better job. I think I want to be a nurse because I like to take care of my sister and cousins when they are sick. I know there are lots of kinds of nurses in hospitals. I might like to take care of babies.

Josh: I don't know what I want to do because I don't think I want to go to college. My grades are bad and I hate school. My parents think I will go to college. I don't know about the options for jobs but I know I want a job where I can make a lot of money.

When many of us were in high school, we did not know what we wanted to do in the future. Even in college, we may still have been unsure about all our options. We know that many of our colleagues completed library school later in life after working in a variety of careers. Teens are expected to have everything all figured out while their brains are still developing. In fact, the human prefrontal cortex, the part of the brain that helps us reason and make rational life decisions, does not fully finish developing until age twenty-five, which is a few years after most students graduate from college and begin what are meant to be their lifelong careers.[17] This means that even the smartest teens with the highest grades will still struggle with reasoning through this process.

HOW CAN LIBRARY STAFF AND OTHER SUPPORTIVE ADULTS HELP TEENS SELECT A CAREER?

A quick internet search for "helping teens select the right career" yields hundreds of articles full of helpful tips. Most of the articles include a combination of the following:

- Treat teens as individuals with unique interests and skills.
- Seek out ways for teens to uncover their hidden strengths and talents.
- In addition to skills, consider a teen's temperament and personality related to a possible career field.
- Help teens select mentors whom they can meet with regularly.
- Expose teens to a variety of activities so they can discover their passions.
- Be encouraging but don't push them—selecting a career takes time.
- Encourage them to do their own research into careers, rather than doing it for them.
- Seek out career and college fairs that will present potential options.
- Help them seek out an after-school or summer job that could help them experience a real workplace, so they can consider in what type of workplace they might enjoy working.

All these tips are terrific, but require a great deal of work from busy adults. After all, each teen must fully embrace the experience for it to be meaningful. For example, we have worked with several teen volunteers and interns who were clearly *not* embracing the volunteer experience at the library. In several of these cases, when asked why they were struggling, they divulged that they did not want to volunteer at the library, but their mom or dad had made them sign up. This situation almost always equals a grumpy teen volunteer showing up and working begrudgingly on projects, which yields little benefit to the teen or the library.

When Amy was at the Teen Desk recently, she spoke with a parent who asked for her help finding books about college scholarships. She guided the mother and daughter to them. She mentioned that there were several current titles that they might want to look at. The mother turned to her daughter, who was looking at her cell phone. Amy could hear the frustration in the mother's voice as she said, "I'm going to need you to be involved here. These books are for you. I've already been to college." In that moment, Amy could tell this was probably not the first time this mother and daughter had discussed college options and likely not the first time the daughter had detached from the process. To assist, Amy grabbed two of the scholarship books and said, "Let's take these over to the table so we can see if one of these guides will be helpful." At the table, she opened one of the books and said, "This one has an index that will help you find scholarships based on personal characteristics, such as having a skill like a musical talent, or based on program of study you are interested in. Do you know what field you might want to study?" At this point, Amy knew she was asking a difficult question, but she was also excited because she was in the process of writing a book about this exact topic. The author in her was jumping with joy, but as a professional librarian she was simply trying to see if the library might have other helpful resources. The mother spoke again: "Well, she likes art, but we want her to consider other options, too."

It is undeniably difficult for parents to help guide their children with all the knowledge they personally have of the world and yet give their children the space to develop their own skills and interests. Supportive adults like parents, teachers, and librarians can offer suggestions, but teens need to be the ones who choose their own careers if they are to take initiative in their classes, and, after they have finished school, in the workplace. We all know people who felt they needed to pursue a particular career path due to familial pressure only to become unhappy adults who switch careers after investing so much in the initial careers they pursued, or drop out of school before graduating.

VOCATIONAL PROGRAMMING FOR PRETEENS

It is never too early to begin talking to students about their goals for the future. With preteens, this discussion does not need to include selecting a college and specific academic program; however, they could already begin informally researching a career by watching videos, reading books, or talking to a professional in this career field. For Amy, this type of informal research helped her decide as a young teen that being a veterinarian was not the right career for her. In middle school, she began volunteering at the animal shelter and was able to talk to a very friendly veterinarian who provided care for the shelter animals. The vet let her sit in on a few procedures after learning that Amy wanted to follow in her footsteps. Amy quickly learned that although she cared deeply for animals, she was not at all interested in the medical aspects of treatments and surgeries, especially the parts involving a bloody scalpel. This firsthand experience helped her to develop a sense of what she wanted to do for a career. Now she is happily employed as a librarian, maintains a home with several pets, has fostered animals, and has volunteered at the local animal shelter as well. Without that experience, she may have followed a pre-med pathway only to struggle and end up in a field that was not the right fit for her.

Many organizations offer volunteer opportunities for students or may welcome a student to visit for a few hours to explore a jobsite. Parents or teachers can help students to get in touch with professionals in their fields of interest. Take-your-child-to-work days are perfect, not only as a way for preteens to bond with parents, but also to interact with career professionals and see a real workplace. Once preteens are legally able to work, summer jobs are an opportunity to start developing personal interests and strengths.

Of course, the library is a terrific place for preteens to begin exploring career options and learn about new and growing fields such as technology and medicine. The program options that we will delve into more fully in later chapters can easily be reformatted slightly and offered to a younger audience. Importantly, if preteens come to see the library as a resource while they are preteens, when they start to think more seriously about how to achieve their career goals, they will be more likely to visit the library and ask a library professional for assistance along the way. This is true for the school library or a local public library; both can serve as a crucial resource for students who are unsure about taking that next step.

HOW LIBRARIES CAN HELP

Libraries can assist teens and preteens as they think about their futures in many important ways:

- by exposing them to the career options available that they might not be aware of

- by helping them discover their passions and skills and encouraging them to explore these through books and electronic resources or participating in programming
- when they are ready, helping them to research careers, colleges, academic programs of study, and possibilities for paying for this coursework

Libraries can provide access to books and online resources so that teens can learn what is available to them. Libraries also employ staff who can help nurture students' talents and ideas so they gain a greater understanding of their potential. All students can benefit from this type of supportive adult figure in their lives, but this type of relationship is especially crucial for students who may not have other adults in their lives who engage them in discussions about their futures. These students especially need our attention to help them complete high school and help them to succeed after graduation.

The Search Institute identifies the External Asset of "Other Adult Relationships" as one of the forty developmental assets that serve as building blocks to help young people grow up to become caring, responsible, and successful adults.[18] This asset provides support to help young people as they navigate the challenges of their preteen and teenage years. Library staff can serve as informal mentors who check in with students and see how things are going for them in school or in their lives outside of school. At the Charlotte Mecklenburg Library's ImaginOn, teen-serving staff members have mentored teens through life crises, including improving their grades, finding a part-time job, or navigating out of abusive relationships. Teens know that staff at ImaginOn are dedicated to assisting them and that they truly care about their success. Whether or not teens have concerned adults in their homes, they may choose to confide in library staff. A positive relationship with a caring adult outside of the home is important in a teen's life when he or she may need our help most.

The libraries where we have worked have offered teens a diverse array of programming topics that can serve to broaden a teen's perspective on the world. Libraries can offer opportunities for teens to explore their interests whether through the library collection or regular programming. The following chapters will cover this in more depth while providing practical tips to library staff members. In addition, libraries often offer volunteer and internship opportunities to teens as young as twelve. Regardless of the profession a teen chooses in the future, this opportunity allows them to experience a workplace and become familiar with customer service, workplace processes, and collaboration. Any volunteer experience can serve to help teens develop an image of a workplace that they may hope to work in one day.

CONCLUSION

The career guidance that is vitally important in a teen's life is often not provided in public schools. Well-intentioned but overburdened guidance counselors simply do not have time to provide individualized career guidance to all 300 or more students assigned to them. This is unfortunate, because vocational programming and access to career guidance and goal planning have been shown to be linked to lower dropout rates and greater college success rates. So where can teens look for career guidance, if not to their school guidance counselors?

In our research, we have found that charter schools, community colleges, parents, and librarians can all help teens develop, focus on, and achieve their career goals. Many community colleges are developing "middle college" programs wherein teens can simultaneously work toward a high school diploma and an associate's degree. These programs have been shown to cost less per student than the cost of enrolling unprepared incoming college freshmen in remedial math and English courses and decrease the risk of dropping out of college. Many of the instructors who participate in these programs act as de facto career guides, informally counseling their students throughout the semester. Parents can act as informal career guides as they provide opportunities for their teens to experience a variety of activities and career options. Frequently, well-intentioned parents bring their teens to library staff when they are looking for volunteer opportunities or college guide books. Once a teen is in the library, we librarians can do so much more to further the career and vocation search. We can offer not only physical materials such as scholarship guides, but also advice through mentorship, vocational experiences through volunteer opportunities and internships, and career exploration through programs such as "Meet a Professional" and "Fast Track: Trade School Fair."

Notes

1. "Student-to-School-Counselor Ratio 2013–2014," American School Counselor Association, https://www.schoolcounselor.org/school-counselors-members.pdf.

2. "WWC Intervention Report," US Department of Education, accessed June 18, 2017, https://ies.ed.gov/ncee/wwc/Docs/InterventionReports/wwc_dual _enrollment_022817.pdf.

3. "Career and College Promise (CCP)," Central Piedmont Community College, www.cpcc.edu/hsprograms.

4. Nancy Hoffman, "Worth the Wait: Early College Comes to Massachusetts," *Jobs for the Future*, February 23, 2017, www.jff.org/blog/2017/02/23/worth-wait-early -college-comes-massachusetts.

5. "Fact Sheet: Expanding College Access Through the Dual Enrollment Pell Experiment," US Department of Education, May 16, 2016, www.ed.gov/news/press -releases/fact-sheet-expanding-college-access-through-dual-enrollment-pell -experiment.

6. Hoffman, "Worth the Wait."

7. "Hot Topics in Higher Education: Reforming Remedial Education," National Conference of State Legislatures, http://www.ncsl.org/documents/educ/ remedialeducation_2013.pdf.

8. Laura Jimenez, Scott Sargrad, Jessica Morales, and Maggie Thompson, "Remedial Education: The Cost of Catching Up," Center for American Progress, September 28, 2016, www.americanprogress.org/issues/education/ reports/2016/09/28/144000/remedial-education/.

9. Emily Deruy, "What Happens When Struggling High-Schoolers Take College Classes," *The Atlantic*, July 14, 2015, www.theatlantic.com/education/ archive/2015/07/college-classes-for-high-school-students/398522/.

10. Louisiana Department of Education, June 20, 2017, www.louisianabelieves.com/ newsroom/news-releases/2017/06/20/jump-start-pre-engineering-career-path way-to-provide-high-school-students-with-advanced-skills-college-credit.

11. *Inside Higher Ed Careers,* May 26, 2017, https://careers.insidehighered.com/ job/1386091/early-college-liaison-academic-program-specialist-hero-high-school/.

12. Emma Sarran Webster, "How This 18-Year-Old Graduated College before High School," *Teen Vogue,* June 12, 2017, www.teenvogue.com/story/18-year-old -graduates-college-before-high-school.

13. Julie Pennell, "Best Colleges Based on Your Astrological Sign," *Teen Vogue,* www .teenvogue.com/gallery/best-colleges-based-on-your-astrological-sign.

14. The Relatives, www.therelatives.org/our-programs/on-ramp-resource-center/.

15. *Say Anything,* directed by Cameron Crowe (1989, Los Angeles, CA: Gracie Films).

16. Find Your Calling, www.findyourcalling.com/.

17. "Understanding the Teen Brain," University of Rochester Medical Center, www .urmc.rochester.edu/encyclopedia/content.aspx?ContentTypeID=1&ContentID =3051.

18. "40 Developmental Assets for Adolescents," Search Institute, www.search-institute .org/content/40-developmental-assets-adolescents-ages-12-18#.

3

How to Get Teens Excited about Career Planning

OW THAT WE HAVE ALL AGREED THAT TEENS AND their parents both need and want career-focused programs in the library, how do we get them excited about attending these events? Anyone who has worked with teens knows that they can be fickle creatures. One day they may enthusiastically attend a library program, and the next day they will want to be left alone. It can be more difficult to engage them in any program that resembles school. We cannot blame them: they have spent seven hours (or more) in school each weekday. They may attend additional tutoring sessions after school or on the weekends. In addition, we must not discredit differences in personalities in teens. As an extrovert, Marie was guilty of occasionally forgetting to step into the shoes of an introvert. After seven hours of forced interaction with their peers, introverted teens may be both physically and mentally exhausted. Falsely assuming everyone is at the same energy level could make the difference in a teen choosing to participate in a group activity versus a self-directed one.

Marie will never forget the day that she was good-naturedly teasing a teen at the library about his unwillingness to participate in an activity. She told him that he was young and should not be "old-man tired." He told her that to get to and from his magnet school he had to get up at 4:45 am and catch a series of three city buses across the county. He was a regular patron of her library because it was near a halfway point bus stop on his afternoon three-bus trip home. Marie felt terrible. Eventually, she and the teen connected and began to chat more and more frequently, and he did participate enthusiasti-cally in one of the library's summer program series. No matter what our teens have faced in the first eight to ten hours of their day, we cannot expect them to be excited about sitting still to listen to a lecture about college choices or college funding in the evening or on a weekend.

A further barrier to engaging teens is the magnetic pull of the screen. Dr. Kathy Koch shared that every minute of every day, YouTube users upload forty-eight hours of new video; Facebook users share 684,478 pieces of infor-mation, Twitter users send over 100,000 tweets, and Instagram users share 3,600 new images.[1] How are we to compete with this? In 2017, we surveyed by e-mail teen-serving library staff from across the country about their cur-rent and projected teen programs related to college-, career-, or vocational-readiness. Many of those who responded mentioned wanting to know how to attract teens to their programs. In this chapter, we will discuss various tried-and-true methods for engaging teens in programs at libraries, including incentives and events so engaging that your teens will not be able to resist attending.

FOOD AND PRIZES

In our experiences, one of the biggest draws for teen participation is food and drink. We have found that the promise of a bag of chips or a piece of candy will draw a group of teens much more quickly than, say, the promise of higher SAT scores or a chance for further education. At one library where we worked, many of our recurring teenage patrons knew that they could ask any Teen Services staff member what they could do for a piece of candy, because they knew that we always kept a stash. In exchange for attempting that week's puzzle or attending that afternoon's program, they were rewarded with something small, such as a piece of gum, a mint, or a Hershey's Kiss. For nearly all our afternoon programs, we offered slightly more robust snacks, such as packs of peanut butter crackers, snack-sized bags of chips, or granola bars.[2] We have seen libraries offer fruit cups or applesauce cups, bananas or apples, or cheese sticks. Although not as healthy, packages of crackers and boxes of chips can be bought in bulk. The healthier options require frequent trips to the store, and leftovers may not stay fresh until your next teen program.[3] With a minimum amount of preparation, you could also buy bags of microwave popcorn for your program. You would simply have to pop a few bags before your program and divide the popcorn into bags or cups. This is an excellent task for a teen volunteer, if you have any. A library system might want to purchase a popcorn machine like those often used at carnivals. This machine can pop greater quantities for large-scale events. After the initial investment to buy the machine, the supplies can be purchased in bulk for a nominal expense.

For beverages, we often shy away from purchasing bottled water. Instead, we would purchase cups (much cheaper per unit) and encourage teens to fill them at water fountains or from pitchers of water we provided. We also encourage teens to bring their own reusable bottles that can be refilled to cut down on the waste created by programs. For larger programs or events, we purchase non-caffeinated soda and juice in containers and provide cups. This method is more budget-friendly, as beverages cost less per ounce in large containers (and water is practically free) and is more ecologically friendly, because teens will not be throwing away empty bottles or cans. Nearly every teen librarian we have spoken to told us that food was the number one draw for teen attendance at programs.

Occasionally we offer a program that has a slightly bigger budget for which we purchase pizza, trays of cookies, or some other more exciting food items. We have often done this for author visits when we hope to draw a crowd of teens to a high-quality program in which they may not initially be interested. At the Beaverton City Library in Oregon, we host a yearly teen program called "Pizza Taste-off" during which teens sample pizza from pizza places around the city and then vote on their favorite. This program has been a huge draw for teens and costs the library very little because all the pizza is generously donated by the restaurants. This program is a time for teens to get to know library staff, socialize, and talk about pizza as if they are restaurant reviewers—what's not to love?

You can tie some of these programs to food. In the summer of 2013, the Charlotte Mecklenburg Library hosted a local culinary school professor at five of its branches for teen programs. The chef-professor shared information about her own schooling, training, career path, and the school at which she taught. She then led the teens in creating their own salsa. The teens enjoyed meeting someone with real-world culinary experience, hearing about the required schooling, and certainly enjoyed the chips and salsa.

Teens will appreciate nearly every giveaway, even if they aren't edible. We have also seen teens enticed to attend a program when promised a free pen or pencil, notebook, book, t-shirt, or flash drive. You are quite likely looking at that list and thinking that your library or branch could never afford such giveaways for your programs. This is where the stuff on the closet shelf comes in handy. We have yet to visit a teen librarian's office and not find a shelf in a cupboard or a closet with a box of small items squirreled away. There may not be a single matched pair of items, and staff may not be sure what to do with some of them. There may be a keychain flashlight from last year's summer reading program, a couple of chunky erasers from a software vendor, a lanyard picked up at the previous year's American Library Association Annual Conference, and a few Advanced Reader Copies of upcoming teen fiction. Simply allow the teens attending your career-focused events to choose an item from the box. The presenters themselves may be able to provide giveaway items. Are you inviting local professionals to speak to your teens? Encourage them to bring a handful of stress balls or flash drives with their company logos on them. Most companies have these sorts of giveaways lying around, and they will be a draw to your program (don't forget to ask the presenter for a few extras to replenish your own stash of giveaways).

A fun anecdote from when we worked at ImaginOn: the teens were quite interested in tattoos and tattoo artistry, so we arranged for a local tattoo artist to visit and share insights from his career. We created flyers to advertise the event and posted them around the teen space. For the two weeks until the program, we answered the same question nearly every day: "Will he be giving away free tattoos?" Teens had come to expect giveaways of small items or snacks at programs and had made the (very hopeful and optimistic) leap to questioning if they might have the opportunity to be tattooed at the library. Even if it wasn't illegal to give tattoos to persons under the age of eighteen in our state, we are pretty sure our library's administration would have frowned upon that particular giveaway. Instead, we gave away hearty snacks and the teens seemed content.[4]

COMPETITIONS

Friendly competition is another suggestion for garnering teen buy-in to your library programs. These competitions can be games of skill, puzzles, or games of chance. A game of skill requires teens to work either alone or in teams to complete a challenge more quickly than another teen or team. Think of a trivia competition. Teams of teens compete against one another to answer questions correctly in the shortest amount of time. A teen librarian could use this same format at the beginning of a career exploration program to build interest in the topic and to establish teens' interest. The presenter(s) could provide some background information on their career or school, or the librarian could do some research to discover background information on the career or school, which could be used to build a short five-question trivia round. After the competition, the teens will be motivated to stay for the full program and learn more about the topics briefly touched upon in the trivia portion. The trivia questions may also trigger further questions from the teens during the program. The puzzle format can be set up in one of two ways: as a timed competition between teens, or as a largely self-directed activity with no winners or losers. Very little staff time is involved in staging these activities. Think, for example, of a scavenger hunt through the stacks. Every teen can participate and come to the same conclusion, and every teen can earn a reward for his or her work. If you have a bigger group of teens who are all ready to participate in the scavenger hunt at the same time, you could increase the competition by encouraging them to race against one another. Perhaps you could have a larger prize for the teen who completes the scavenger hunt the most quickly, with the most correct answers.

When looking specifically at vocational-readiness program ideas, a teen-serving library employee could create a simple scavenger hunt that would direct teens to look at books and online information about vocations. When creating a scavenger hunt, keep in mind its difficulty level and the length of time required to complete it. You do not want the hunt to go on so long that teens will give up in the middle, nor do you want it to be so easy that their intelligence is insulted. If you are planning to direct participants to specific titles in your collection, make sure that you have extra copies in case the target title is checked out by a patron. Because we worked in a library with a floating collection, we would often request two or three copies of each target title the week before we set up the scavenger hunt and would keep the extra copies in our offices, ready to be shelved as needed to replace any copies that were checked out. You could direct teens to a specific Dewey decimal number or section of numbers so that you do not have to check every day to make sure that certain titles are on the shelf. Keep in mind accessibility: do

not ask teens to complete tasks that would be impossible or extremely difficult for someone living with a disability.

You could also ask teens to complete a challenge or activity that would
allow them to try out job-seeking or vocational tasks. For example, you could
have a group of teens see who can correctly tie a tie in the shortest amount
of time. Yes, this would work with a co-ed group of teens. You could provide
handouts that walk the teens through tie-tying; show a video clip explaining how to knot a tie or allow the teens to use their phones or other mobile
devices for tips and tricks. If the group seems reasonably adept at tying ties,
you could increase the challenge by asking them to tie a Windsor knot or a
bow tie. In a large group, teams of teens could collaborate for the challenge.
You may be wondering where you will find the budget for purchasing ties.
There is no need to purchase any. Because (in theory) the ties won't sustain
any damage, you can ask for one-day loans from your coworkers or their
spouses. Perhaps you could purchase one fun tie to use as a prize.

Another very soft form of competition is the raffle. Participants are given
numbered tickets for drawings to win prizes. A duplicate of each ticket is
placed in a receptacle. At some point during the event or program, an event
organizer draws a ticket from the receptacle, and the owner of the corresponding ticket wins a prize. These are most often conducted during larger
programs or events, such as vocational school fairs or career days. When
deciding to put on a raffle, you should include that information on your promotional materials. If your library's budget allows you to purchase prizes or
giveaways, we recommend purchasing items that tie into the theme of the
program. In the past, we have purchased such items as career aptitude guide-
books and scholarship guidance books, along with the requisite candy.

If your library does not have a large budget for programs, or if you are
restricted from purchasing prizes, you could work with other organizations in
your area to provide giveaways in exchange for advertising. You could ask the
local pizza parlor for coupons for free pizza in exchange for placing its logo on
your promotional materials, for example, or you could ask the participating
schools at your expo for giveaways. Museums and other cultural institutions
in your area may be happy to provide a set of tickets as a giveaway. We often
bundle up advanced reader copies of upcoming new teen releases with fancy
ribbon and maybe add a movie theater-sized candy box and teens are thrilled
with these prizes. If your library receives Advanced Reader's Copies, this is a
great use for them after library staff have reviewed the titles. Raffles are also

a useful way to entice participants to stay and explore your event more thoroughly. You could distribute raffle tickets at the beginning of the event and tell participants that the drawing will occur in an hour and that they must be present to win. Raffles can provide an incentive for attending your program at little or no cost to the library.

HANDS-ON ACTIVITIES

As mentioned earlier, teens are not likely to want to sit still and listen to a presenter after being in school all day. A good way to combat this resistance is to involve the teen participants in a hands-on activity or program. The teens won't be required to keep completely still and focused. The "maker movement" is alive and well, and works with many vocational exploration programs. If you have access to a makerspace, programs that teach how to use the software and equipment in that space would certainly be a vocational or career-ready training opportunity. In a makerspace that is part of the Charlotte Mecklenburg Library system, there are computers with a variety of computer-aided drafting and 3-D design software installed. Teens can participate in programs in this space where they learn to utilize the software to create everything from 3-D models of items related to their favorite fandoms to fidget spinners to personalized cell phone cases. Through the process, they gain valuable foundational knowledge of simple 3-D design or computer-aided drafting programs, and familiarity with the language and terminology used in 3-D printing. This information will serve them well if they choose to pursue vocational training in computer- or engineering-related programs post-high school.

During her shift in the makerspace, Marie spoke with several users. One was a young teen, barely twelve, who had created his own brand logo and was excited to make vinyl stickers to apply to his various belongings. They talked further as she assisted him with putting the logo into the correct software program to prepare it for the vinyl cutter. She learned that he has been making bow ties since he was nine years old. He first gave, and then sold, them, to his classmates, friends, and families. He had built a loyal fan base. People knew that they could come to him for custom bow ties at a quick turnaround. Now that he was turning twelve, he started crafting his custom bow ties for customers from wood (cut on the library's laser cutter) and fabric. He now sells his bow ties for a profit. This young teen is getting more vocational-readiness information and training via library programs where he learned more about how to use the laser cutter, vinyl cutter, and associated software than he might receive in his four years of high school. As he continues to mature, he may also take advantage of our library's programs on creating and sustaining a self-owned business.

A teen librarian working for the Mount Prospect Public Library in Illinois runs a maker program of sorts for his teen patrons. Although his library does not have a physical makerspace, he creates opportunities for teens to regularly get their hands on many different pieces of hardware and software, including 3-D printers, Makey Makeys, Arduinos, robotics, circuitry, and stop motion video production. He shared:

> Most of the programming we do is informational and instructional activities on a practical level for people who want to learn techniques and skills to improve and enhance their ability to do their jobs at work, school, at home, and beyond. That is learning that will enable . . . students with reinforcement for what they are learning in school so that they will be effective when they eventually enter the world of work. . . We design the programs with activities that teach in a fun and entertaining manner so people will have a good time learning . . . our activities are designed to encourage critical and analytical thinking, problem solving, manual dexterity, eye-hand coordination, teamwork and social skills, etc.[5]

Even without access to a full makerspace, you can still provide hands-on programs that will get teens excited about trying different vocations. In Charlotte, North Carolina, there is an option for homeschooling families to receive visits from various vocation-themed vans to help families provide their teens with exposure to these types of programs. We spoke with one homeschooling mother who told us about her teenaged daughter's experience with a cosmetology van. She shared that the daughter had shown no interest in cosmetology and self-identified as a tomboy who wanted nothing to do with beauty school. The mother told us that the cosmetology program was the only one in the area at the time, and that she knew the importance of continually exposing her children to these opportunities. After an afternoon exploring a wide range of cosmetology basics, the teen daughter ended up enjoying the activity. She is still sure that she will not be going to cosmetology school after high school, but she gained a new appreciation for the vocation, and is now able to give concrete reasons for not pursuing the program further. Teen librarians can provide this same opportunity within our branches, even if we are not experts in the field. You could check out the many nail art books available in your system and provide those, plus nail polish, to teens to experiment with a form of cosmetology. In a later chapter, we will discuss hosting professionals in vocational fields, and encouraging those presenters to bring hands-on demonstrations to the library.

Not every vocational-readiness program needs to be a boring recitation of training and schooling options. These programs can also be practical and enjoyable, and allow students to really get their hands on the information and try out the various options.

GROUP PRESENTATIONS

Sometimes your library may be fortunate enough to be host to a captive audience. School media centers can invite groups of students to the library during the school day for whole-class vocational-readiness programs. Public libraries may host school groups, day camps, or other youth groups who visit for scheduled field trips. These groups would be excellent audiences for career exploration-type programs. In talking with teen-serving library staff across the country, many said programs with captive audiences have the highest attendance and often the highest engagement levels from the teens in attendance. Some librarians reported working with nearby public schools to coordinate dates and times, and mentioned how helpful it was to have the schools send out reminder blasts via text or e-mail to the students and their families.

Other librarians shared that they would invite local youth-serving organizations to bring their teens to the library for a program if they had transportation.[6] In our own careers, we have also gone to visit the sites of local youth-serving organization such as Boys & Girls Clubs to provide library programming on everything from SAT prep to vision-boarding to information about vocational schools. In addition, we have provided vocational programming for teens with disabilities who were excited to learn about career options. We will cover these partnership opportunities in more detail in chapter[8], but they are worth mentioning here because they do provide a guaranteed captive audience for the programs that you will develop. Furthermore, once a relationship has been developed, you can use those open lines of communication between organizations to promote future vocation-related programs.

USING TEEN FEEDBACK TO PLAN PROGRAMS

A sometimes-overlooked means of discovering which library programs are attractive to teens is the teens themselves. Teen feedback can give a teen-serving library staffer a wealth of information about the best times to plan programs, how to excite teens, and how to attract them. If you have worked with teens for any length of time, you will know that once they are comfortable with you, they will share (and perhaps over-share) all their opinions with you. If your teen population is not yet at the sharing stage of the relationship, library staff can still gather feedback through observation or formal surveys that allow teens to share their responses anonymously.

When possible, it is ideal to gather teen feedback directly from them. Listen to your teens and what they ask for, both directly or indirectly. A teen may ask for information about how to format a resume, but not be aware that he should also ask about the proper attire for an interview. Reference questions are an excellent way to gauge teens' interest in a subject. We suggest that you keep either an electronic or paper record of the types of questions that teen patrons ask, and tailor your programs to those interests and needs.

A teen librarian at the Pueblo City-County Library in Pueblo, Colorado, takes teen feedback one step further. Her library has a robust Teen Advisory Board (TAB) that plans all its teen programs. She shared with us that her teens "do not express interest in very structured programs and prefer things that don't feel like school." Furthermore, her library's teen program attendance has grown by 200 percent over the previous year because of the teens themselves independently steering and planning the programs.[7] Your library does not need to go to the extreme of allowing teens to plan 100 percent of your programs, but you could certainly form a TAB or Teen Library Council (TLC) and allow your teens to assist in planning some of your programs. This creates buy-in from teen patrons. When they have helped to plan the program, they will be proud of it and excited to attend. They will also help you to spread the word to other teens. The teens who had the idea to have the program initially are a guaranteed audience for your program. At many libraries, there is an added incentive for teens who participate in their TAB. At the library staff's discretion, participation could count as a service activity, and any teen who needs to earn service hours for school or extracurriculars could participate on a TAB to earn those hours.

It is essential to collect feedback from your patrons prior to investing time, energy, and finances in programs, resources, and equipment. Recently, we attended a presentation by Georgia Coleman, Customer Service Director of South Carolina's Richland Public Library. She shared an anecdote about the development of the new makerspace at the main library. During the design phase, the planning team repeatedly heard from other libraries and maker-spaces and read in articles that a library makerspace needed 3-D printers. The team prepared to purchase 3-D printers, but first decided to solicit feed-back from the community that would be using the space. A local artist was contracted to survey other members of the artistic community of Columbia, South Carolina, to discern what types of equipment they would like to see in the space. She also asked what types of programs the community would be interested in. The results of the survey were surprising to the planning team: in the end, the artistic community and library patrons overwhelmingly called for fiber arts, woodworking, and microbusiness development. Many members of the community, especially women, were beginning to learn to use power tools to do woodworking, and then selling their products via Etsy .com. They desired instruction in the tools' use, and guidance in cultivating their microbusinesses. Although this example focuses on a very large project meant to engage both teens and adults, it still applies to program planning designed exclusively for teens. It illustrates how essential it is to interact with your constituents and listen to them, and not rely wholly upon articles and other libraries' feedback in your planning. What works for one library may not work for another. Although it is excellent to begin by reading articles and books, you should then survey your community to narrow down your ideas. Without this survey, the Richland Public Library would have spent funds on 3-D printers, software to run them, and staff training, and most of the public would have ignored the printers. Thanks to the survey, the library could focus its makerspace development on what truly mattered to the community.[8] To help you do something similar, appendix A includes a sample workshop eval-uation that you can edit and tailor for your own needs.

TEEN-LED CAREER WORKSHOPS

The next step after soliciting advice from your teen patrons is to ask them to lead the programs. In a *School Library Journal* blog post, Jennifer Velasquez calls for an end to Teen Advisory Boards that engage teens in an adviso-ry-only capacity and instead calls for putting teens in charge of programs. She makes the point that simply asking teens for advice is passive; instead, we should be encouraging them to participate actively in teen programs by facilitating them or even leading them. In the post, she emphasizes the need to engage your "regulars," the teens who come to your library often, regardless of the day's program offering. Listen to these teens and plan your programs to engage them.[9] When they are excited about the programs at the library, they will tell their friends at school and other extracurricular activities about the library, and your teen patron base will grow.

Many respondents to our survey defined a successful or popular library program as one that the teens themselves have planned, presented, led, and/ or asked for directly. One anonymous respondent wrote that a successful program is one where "you get at least two or more teens that learn something new and are excited."[10] In the survey and in our conversations with teen librarians across the country, we heard overwhelmingly that above all else, those who serve teens in libraries must remain flexible and open to what their patrons desire. Furthermore, by allowing the teens to assist in program planning, we're providing them with leadership opportunities. Just think: they may end up in a job interview, discussing their experience "working" with librarians at their local library, describing how they lead programs. This might give them the edge they need to earn employment, which allows your programs to come full circle to success.

If you are not comfortable allowing teens to fully lead programs, you can still solicit their opinions. Many programming staff at libraries utilize the website Pinterest to plan their programs. It is an absolute wealth of program and craft ideas. Before you begin purchasing materials for a project or reserving your community room for a program, check with your teens. Show them your "Library Programs" Pinterest board and see which Pins get them excited. You can also use pop-up programming, which is unplanned and not on a program calendar, to test programs on smaller groups of teens before planning for the main event. One of our former libraries used to do a pop-up program whenever we had a group of teens in the space who did not have homework to do and no other library activities were on the calendar. We would pull out materials from an earlier program, or simply gather the teens for an informal discussion. If we had a program on Monday where teens made cards to donate to a children's hospital and only a few teens attended, we can pull out those same materials on Thursday when a group of teens gather to hang out in the library. This same sort of pop-up program can be used to test an idea before officially planning and promoting an event.

STEM toys are perfect for pop-up programs because you can simply bring out the technology and let the teens develop the program on the spot. For example, we recently brought a Sphero (www.sphero.com) into the teen room and started driving it around and through the computer desks. The teens started looking at what we were doing, and so we invited them to try driving it. A few enthusiastically jumped up to try. Not twenty minutes later, the teens had created an elaborate maze using school supplies we had lying around the teen desk and were working together to problem-solve how to work their way through the maze. The most difficult part was gaining enough momentum to travel over a ramp created using bookends. This program took very little planning on our part yet resulted in an hour of fun for a bunch of teens, some of whom were initially reluctant to participate until they saw that their peers were basically leading the program.

The Young Adult Library Services Association (YALSA) Teen Programming Guide also addresses teen-led programming. YALSA recommends a youth-adult partnership approach to program development, engaging teens via outreach to local schools, involving teens in every step of the programming process, using a flexible participatory design model to allow teens to modify and adapt programs to better meet their needs, facilitating rather than leading programs, and enabling teens to engage in peer-to-peer learning activities.[11]

To reach these recommendations, YALSA partly relied on Hart's Ladder, which is a visual representation of the various levels of involvement that teens may have in programs.[12] The goal is to climb as high on the ladder as possible, with the top rung being achieved when "young people and adults share decision making: young people have the ideas, set up the project and invite adults to join them in making decisions throughout the process."[13] The very bottom of the ladder contains three rungs that are totally nonparticipatory for teens: manipulation, decoration, and tokenism. On these three rungs, teens are given little or no voice during the program and are not consulted beforehand. At the bottom-most rung, teens may even be taken advantage of. The top five rungs of the ladder are all considered participatory to varying degrees, and are what teen-serving staff should aim for in program planning. When planning your program, look at Hart's Ladder (figure 3.1) and ask yourself which rung the program aligns with. Is there anything that you can change about the program plan to move it higher up the ladder?

FIGURE 3.1

Roger Hart's Ladder of Young People's Participation

Rung 8: Young people and adults share decision-making

Rung 7: Young people lead and initiate action

Rung 6: Adult-initiated, shared decisions with young people

Rung 5: Young people consulted and informed

Rung 4: Young people assigned and informed

Rung 3: Young people tokenized*

Rung 2: Young people are decoration*

Rung 1: Young people are manipulated*

Non-participation

*Note: Hart explains that the last three rungs are *nonparticipation.*

Adapted from Hart, R. (1992). *Children's Participation from Tokenism to Citizenship.* Florence: UNICEF Innocenti Research Center.

Finally, we would be remiss if we didn't also mention teen-led program promotion. There is no marketing technique more powerful with teens than peer-to-peer promotion. Encourage your teen interns, volunteers, and teen regulars to post the library's flyers to their personal Instagram and Facebook accounts. Encourage them to take pictures during events and tag them with your library's hashtag. Teen volunteers or interns who are interested in art or graphic design can help you design flyers that will appeal to teens. If libraries must follow style guidelines, teens can be shown how to adhere to these guidelines while still creating an eye-catching flyer or image to post digitally.

Often, if you can convince one or two teens to attend a program, you can convince them to bring their friends. There have been times when we've convinced one teen to attend a program by promising snacks and a good time, and then watched him tell his buddies (often via text) that they need to come too. We are always happy to welcome these additional teens to our programs. We teen librarians often bemoan the strong peer pressure on teens today; however, we can leverage this to our advantage and promote peer-to-peer excitement about library programs.

CONCLUSION

As library staff, we know that teens can benefit from vocational-focused programs at the library. Yet the question looms large: how do we pique their interest in our vocational-focused programs, which may not at first glance appear as fun and glamorous as some of our other programs? We have found that offering snacks and giveaways at programs raises attendance. Furthermore, friendly competition entices teens to check out what we have to offer. Hands-on activities during vocational programming help teens remain engaged, which often means they leave with more information than they would from programs that do not offer opportunities for interaction with the program topic.

Most importantly, it all comes back to the teens themselves. We must engage with our teen audience and discover what sorts of programs it truly wants and needs. Once we learn this, we can move on to looking at teen feedback to plan and execute teen-led programs in partnership with our youth. Once we have the program plan in place, we can then rely heavily on teen peer-to-peer marketing to promote these programs. The programs that teens have helped to initiate and plan will more often be well-attended because they have teen buy-in. Teens will be excited to talk about these programs with their peers, and they will want to attend the program when they know that they have helped to make this program come to life. Even if you think teen vocational programming sounds like it will elicit blank looks from your teens, there are many ways to make it more exciting. The remaining chapters in this book will cover specific programs that we have found that teens enjoyed. We always love it when teens ask, "When can we do that again?" When we hear that during a vocational program we know we have done something right!

Notes

1. Kathy Koch, *Screens and Teens: Connecting with Our Kids in a Wireless World* (Chicago: Moody Publishers, 2015).
2. We are aware that peanut butter is often a banned item in many libraries and schools. If this is the case, simply substitute cheese crackers, or omit crackers altogether. Teens are usually knowledgeable about their own allergies, so even if peanut butter is not explicitly banned, it is a good practice to ask the group if there are any allergy sufferers, and if so, to omit the crackers for that day.
3. We have heard of a unique case where a public library was located directly across the street from a public high school. The public library teen services staff fostered

a partnership with the public high school principal and were permitted to retrieve leftover food from the school cafeteria to serve to teens who attended their library programs after school. This allowed the library to offer healthy options, such as fresh-cut fruits and vegetables and cheese sticks, at no cost. The school thus avoided throwing away edible food and the teen services staff often visited the school to lead programs or activities for the student body, along with food collection visits.

4. "Tattooing and Body Piercing. State Laws, Statutes and Regulations," National Conference of State Legislatures, August 1, 2017, www.ncsl.org/research/health/tattooing-and-body-piercing.aspx.

5. Lawrence A. D'Urso, "RE: Teen Vocational Programs Survey Follow-Up," personal communication to Marie Harris, May 19, 2017.

6. Teen Vocational Programs at Libraries (April 26, 2017), survey distributed by ALA Editions.

7. Ibid.

8. Georgia Coleman, "Richland County Library Customer Service Mode," Minutes of the Charlotte Mecklenburg Library Public Service Managers Meeting, July 27, 2017, Beatties Ford Road Library, Charlotte, NC.

9. Jennifer Velasquez, "The Trouble with Teen Programming," *School Library Journal*, October 15, 2014.

10. Teen Vocational Programs at Libraries (April 26, 2017), survey distributed by ALA Editions.

11. Young Adult Library Services Association, "YALSA Teen Programming Guidelines" 2017, www.ala.org/yalsa/teen-programming-guidelines.

12. "Hart's Ladder," www.myd.govt.nz/documents/engagement/harts-ladder.pdf.

13. Ibid.

The "Meet a Professional" Workshop Series

F YOU TELL TEENS AT YOUR LIBRARY YOU ARE HOSTING A career workshop series where they will be able to meet a professional and find out about a specific job field, you are likely to see some eye rolling. The series is not an immediate sell to teens; however, with a little work to make this series appealing for teens at your location, these programs can be a huge success. For this chapter, we are using our experiences planning and facilitating this type of career program series at the Charlotte Mecklenburg Library. However, we believe this series could be adapted to any library system across the country. The program series thrives when teens are given the chance to provide feedback and to help select the careers they find interesting. Library staff use this feedback to sculpt the series and to market it as well.

This chapter will provide you with ideas for professionals to include in this program series, tips for selecting presenters, an outline for the workshops, and tips for connecting teens with additional resources after the program.

THE IMPORTANCE OF MEETING CAREER PROFESSIONALS

"Often the most current information about a career field, especially in a specific geographic location, may not be available online or in books. The best information comes from people who are actually working in that career field."[1] Career counselors recommend that teens conduct informational interviews with professionals in fields that interest them. Informational interviews are meant to provide insider information about a specific career or industry. Such interviews can yield the following benefits for teens or young adults:

- Provide an insider's view of what it is like to work in that career field or at a specific company or organization.
- Learn what education, certifications, or job training will be needed to enter this field as well as what skills may be useful for success in this career field.
- Broaden their view of the career field by learning about jobs they may not have considered previously.
- Gain an understanding of what employers in this field may be looking for, which will help when applying for and interviewing for jobs.
- Form a relationship with someone already working in the field of interest (which may possibly lead to a longer-term mentorship opportunity).

Certainly, the benefits of meeting with a professional in a field of interest are numerous. Yet, how are teens to set up an informational interview, especially with a career professional in a field that may not be very prominent in their community? Teens living in smaller towns have fewer opportunities to interact with career professionals from a broad range of fields. For example, a teen who is artistically talented might never consider a career in graphic design if she has no interaction with someone in that field. She might consider careers that her parents have more familiarity with although she might instead have started on a path to becoming a successful and fulfilled graphic designer if she knew more about careers in this field. Libraries can help bridge this gap for teens and connect them with professionals from a broad range of career fields.

During an "I Can Be a Photographer" program at the Charlotte Mecklenburg Library, a teen attended who was deeply engaged and asked many questions of our guest photographer. We noticed that after the session, this teen stayed to chat with our presenter. He also asked, "Do you ever need someone to assist you on shoots? I've been photographing for a while, but I am looking to try other types of photography, including fashion photography." He pulled up a website on his phone to show our presenter his work. The presenter stayed to talk to the teen. He said he was not hiring right now, but that sometimes he did need extra assistance or could invite the teen along to observe the shoot. He said that the teen photographer "would need to just watch and not take any pictures, but it would be good experience." The photographer mentioned that the teen could bring his parents so they could learn more about what it is like to be a photographer. The presenter then gave the teen a business card and asked him to follow up by e-mail. This teen had taken the initiative to learn skills needed to be successful in the field of photography. He was already practicing networking and was comfortable showing off his work. We were impressed by him, but also talked about the fact that the library had made this interaction possible. The library connected this passionate teen to a resource that he was not sure how to connect to previously.

As adults, we probably know how important it can be to have a career mentor—someone who can not only share his or her own personal experience working in a certain field, but also provides encouragement and constructive feedback and point out opportunities we may otherwise miss. Teens can benefit immensely from a relationship with a career mentor, especially if they already have a passion for a certain field. *Teen Vogue* advises, "A mentor takes a personal interest in your ambitions, and what's important is that you put time and energy into a relationship with someone who genuinely cares about your career trajectory."[2]

IDEAS FOR CAREER PROFESSIONALS WITH TEEN APPEAL

Teens regularly interact with teachers, counselors, doctors, coaches, and other professionals. They already have an idea of what those careers might be like. They probably know a bit about the career fields in which their parents work, too. However, what are the career fields about which teens in your community have limited or no information? Do your teens have interests that could translate into careers? These are all important questions to get you started when thinking about hosting a career series of this type at your location.

The list below is in no way comprehensive, but includes suggestions from teens we have worked with and many of the professionals we have hosted as part of this workshop series over the years.

- tattoo artist
- salon owner or stylist
- magazine editor
- sports trainer
- physical therapist
- journalist
- photographer
- artist (all media)
- dancer, yoga/fitness instructor, or professional athlete
- writer
- recording artist
- fashion designer or stylist
- business owner
- app or website designer
- engineer
- music therapist
- vet tech
- contractor
- nurse
- restaurant owner
- baker or chef
- animal trainer
- environmental scientist
- mechanic
- nutritionist

Speaking with the teens you work with will help you create a list of careers from which to begin. If your library hosts a Teen Library Council or Teen Advisory Group, it can help in planning these workshops. This is beneficial not only because their feedback will help you plan programs, but also because teens are more likely to be invested in these programs and to show up if they feel some ownership over the series.

It may work best to ask teens about their interests rather than the career they are interested in for a few reasons:

- Some teens may not know what they want to do as a career after high school.
- Teens may think they want to be doctors or teachers because that is what they are familiar with, but they might not know about other options available that they may enjoy as a career. Remember that this whole series is about opening their eyes to what is out there.
- Teens might be unaware that their interests could be turned into viable career paths.

The next step is to set about locating professionals to speak at your library. We will provide some tips for this process later in the chapter.

VETTING YOUR CAREER PROFESSIONALS

Not all successful career professionals are engaging public speakers. If you add in the fact that the audience will be a group of possibly cynical twelve– to eighteen-year-olds who have been sitting in hard plastic chairs all day in a classroom, you must ensure that program speakers are not only knowledgeable, but also engrossing, dynamic, and know how to roll with the punches. Therefore, in planning career series programs in the past, we have always selected our speakers carefully. We either meet them ourselves around the community (at various meetings or networking events) or solicit a recommendation from a friend, colleague, or family member.

For example, last year we hosted an "I Can Be a Pharmacy Technician" event based on a recommendation from a colleague. You will notice that pharmacy technician is not on the list of careers with teen appeal above. Initially, we were not sure how successful this would be, but our colleague met this individual and raved about his charisma and ability to connect with youth. It turns out teens loved our presenter and were deeply engaged throughout the program. Teens reported they had not considered becoming a pharmacist or pharmacy technician as a possible career until this program; in fact, many had not known what a pharmacist did. The presenter's skill in speaking to teens and his enthusiasm for his career were essential to the success of this program.

Do not be shy about asking the selected professional to bring hands-on examples of their work to share with your teen patrons. When our tattoo artist visited, he brought a tattoo machine (sans needles) and let the teens pass it around to look at and feel its heft. (Additionally, our tattoo artist taught everyone, including library staff, that only novices and outsiders to the field refer to these as "tattoo guns." To professionals, they are "tattoo machines.") When skateboard shop owners visited, they brought multiple skateboard models and parts for the teens to handle (but not ride). They also brought giveaways for teens like posters, t-shirts, and stickers—all of which are items that shop owners tend to accumulate because companies regularly send free promotional items to stores. When we hosted a photographer, he brought several DSLR cameras for teens to test out. The painter who visited brought some of her canvases as well as her favorite set of brushes to pass around. An opportunity for teens to handle tools of specific trades can make the program feel more interactive and less like a lecture. They set the stage for teens to feel comfortable and engaged, especially during the Q & A portion of the program.

We have never paid a professional for presenting at one of our career workshops. We have found that community members are often flattered to be invited to speak to teens about their careers and feel that they are giving back by supporting youth who may enter their career fields in the future. Some professionals who work for companies or organizations in the community receive permission to present the workshop during the workday because their company considers it to be an outreach effort. Of course, entrepreneurs and other independent professionals may not be receiving payment for their time. For this reason, we always try to make them feel welcome and appreciated. You can do this by being prepared for the program, greeting them at the front door, offering water and a small snack for them, marketing the program to ensure a good turnout, and thanking them in person when they leave and then again by e-mail after the program. If we take pictures at the program, we often send the presenter a link to the photos so he or she will have a memento of the visit. This helps the library to develop advocates in the community—and we all know we can never have too many library advocates!

OUTLINE FOR "MEET A PROFESSIONAL" WORKSHOP SERIES

Introduction
During this portion of the workshop, a library staff member welcomes teens to the program and introduces the speaker. It is also useful to let teens know about the format for the workshop, including whether the speaker will take questions throughout the program or at the end.

Overview of Career
The speaker will present a description of his or her career field. This likely includes what a typical day or week is like and what type of work environment can be expected from that field.

Journey to This Career Path
The speaker will provide an overview of the path to becoming a professional in this field, including what inspired him or her to pursue this career.

Education Required
The speaker will share information about what education is required to be successful in this field. This may include classes, internships, or other training.

Challenges Involved

We ask our speakers to be honest with teens about the challenges they face in their career fields. What makes for a tough day for them? Where have they struggled to be successful? What sorts of struggles can people new to the field expect to work to overcome?

Rewards of the Career Field

To counter the challenges, we also want our speakers to share what it is they love about their chosen careers and what inspires them along the way. What makes a good workday? What keeps them working towards their career goals? We encourage them to give teens examples of times when they felt real success, rather than merely providing an overview. When professionals talk about their achievements, it tends to illustrate their passion to those listening.

Related Careers in This Field

If teens have an interest in this area, what are other related careers they could pursue? What are their options for succeeding in this field? For example, a vet technician might talk about some of the careers they know their classmates went into after graduating from the same vet tech program.

What Teens Can Do Now if They Are Interested in This Field

How should teens prepare now if they have an interest in this field? We want teens to have an accurate idea of what sort of work and preparation they should be engaging in for future success. For example, if they want to become video game designers, they can be seeking out graphic design and coding classes at their high schools, or in after-school experiences. As they approach graduation, they can begin researching which local schools offer a video game designer associate's degree program.

Questions from Teens

We leave plenty of time for teens to ask questions and gain a deeper understanding of this career option. Teens come up with all sorts of questions that the adults running the program probably would not think of. You might also develop a couple questions ahead of time, in case you need to get the discussion started. Sometimes all the teens are waiting for someone else to go first so this takes some pressure off them.

MARKETING YOUR "MEET A PROFESSIONAL" WORKSHOP SERIES

The success of a "Meet a Professional" workshop series at your library may depend on your efforts to market the program series. We believe it helps if programs of this type are part of a regularly occurring series. It is more appealing to teens and parents if your library plans to feature several career options, rather than just one or two. Some teens may only attend the workshops featuring careers in which they are already interested, but you may find that some teens will attend almost all the workshops, which we think makes this series even more beneficial for them. Hosting the programs in a series is also a boon to your marketing. You can tell interested teens or parents that every first Wednesday of the month you'll have a Meet a Professional program, and build a following.

You might want to call your series something like, "Meet a Professional: [name of the career]" or "I Can Be a [name of the career]" so that the topic of the program is clear to your audience. If teens in your community tend to be interested in programs that help them prepare for their futures, or if the parents of teens in your community tend to be the ones picking up your program flyers and bringing their children to the library for programs, a straightforward name for these programs might result in more success. However, if you feel it might be more difficult to sell a career program series to teens in your community, then you can create more appealing titles for your programs. For example, a staff member at ImaginOn offered a monthly career program series she called "Lucrative Pop Culture" because she wanted to emphasize to teens that they could earn a lot of money if they put some effort into pursuing a specific career goal. She invited professionals such as radio DJs, a reality TV star, and a professional painter, along with plenty of other engaging professionals to speak at these programs.

You might choose to title each program individually. Here are some examples:

- *Hot Kicks: Do You Have What It Takes to Be a Shoe Designer?*
  Meet Matt LeStrange, shoe designer at Nike, and learn what it takes to be a professional shoe designer.

- *Walk the Runway: Fashion Photography*
  Interested in the field of fashion or photography? Meet April Smith, a professional model turned fashion photographer and stylist.

• *Cooking Challenge with Chef Craig*
Learn about what it's like to work in a fancy restaurant as the head chef. We will end the program with a fun cooking challenge.

Teachers and guidance counselors are often excited to hear that the library is offering a program to help teens think about future careers. They may put up flyers in their schools, pass out flyers to students, or promote library programs during school announcements. Some schools have newsletters that they send home to families as paper copies, e-mails, and voicemails. This is a great way to reach parents or students who may not already know about what your library offers. Connecting with staff at the schools in your community can help you brainstorm career workshops that might interest students, especially if your local schools have any type of career program, such as a CTE (Career Technical Education) class. If your school system features a magnet school or career pathway program, your library may want to feature a few workshops in a related career.

Are there nonprofits in your community that serve teens? Youth-serving nonprofits are often looking for a way to introduce teens to career options. Libraries are allies in assisting the teens in your community, and a career program series is a great opportunity to form partnerships. In Charlotte, the staff at the Goodwill Career Leadership Academy for Youth (CLAY) were always happy to hear about the career programs we had to offer for teens and would sometimes make field trips to the library with their teen participants. The same was true of On Ramp, a youth-serving nonprofit in Charlotte that works to prepare teens and young adults for the next step in their future. If you have any connections with the staff who work in these programs, or with the career counselors at a career-based magnet school, it is well worth your time to reach out to them and discover if there is a specific day or time during which they can take after-school field trips and then plan your Meet a Professional series programs for those times. These were terrific partnerships that helped us to increase the number of participants in our programs and deepen the level of engagement of the teens attending each workshop.

Although this has been mentioned in previous chapters, it bears briefly repeating that you should consider your audience when marketing, and be prepared to market innovatively. At ImaginOn, we would make use of Instagram to market to our teens. As many teens do not follow the library directly on social media, we would create posts and then ask teen volunteers or regular patrons to like and share the posts. We also made sure to always make our flyers appealing to teens. Maybe you have a staff member who has an interest in graphic design, or maybe a teen intern or member of the Teen Library Council who wants to build up his or her skills and can help create flyers. Eye-catching flyers on tables in the teen area and quarter-sheets to hand out to teens and parents have worked well for this program series.

In addition, there are many ways to make your workshops engaging and exciting for teens attending. Some of these ideas include hands-on activities, competitions, giveaways, and snacks. Check out chapter[3], How to Get Teens Excited about Career Planning, for additional ideas.

FOLLOWING UP WITH TEENS TO CONNECT THEM WITH RELATED RESOURCES

It is important to follow up with teens who attend your programs and show interest in a topic. There are several ways to get this information to teens. You should plan to have some related resources available at the program itself, of course. Meet a Professional may draw in some attendees who are new to your library, and so you will want to have program calendars and flyers for upcoming related programs available. In Charlotte, North Carolina, our library system hosts a successful annual series of programs relating to preparation for college or university entrance. At every Meet a Professional program we would be sure to tell the teens and their parents about this resource, and to mention specific upcoming programs at nearby branches.

A book display featuring books about the career being discussed can be set up in the meeting/community room where you are hosting the program. You could also prepare bookmarks with a list of suggested reading to pass out at the end of the program, which reminds teens that you are happy to help them locate additional information. Alternatively, the bookmark could feature related (and vetted) websites that students could visit to learn more. Although we library staff members are skilled at research, you do not need to rely on research alone to create these displays or bookmarks; visiting professionals will be able to advise you of websites that they like to frequent for their own professional development or recommend books that they found inspiring.

Some libraries' policies will allow for the collection of names and phone numbers or e-mail addresses at programs. If you can do so, you could ask the participants to sign in on their way out, and to indicate if they would like to receive further information. This allows you to send out e-mails with expanded information based upon the questions teens asked at the end of the programs.

The library has access to so many useful resources, including e-books, articles, books, and videos. Some libraries also subscribe to Lynda.com or another online learning interface where teens can watch videos and practice to acquire skills. Even if your library does not have a subscription to Lynda .com, there are how-to guides, YouTube, and other free resources like Khan Academy that library staff can recommend. We can help teens find information about internships, camps, and other educational programs that will set them on the path towards a career goal.

CONCLUSION

If you have been considering adding career-planning programs to what you offer at your library, we recommend some sort of "Meet a Professional" program series. This series exposes teens to careers they may not have considered, and the best part is that you can base these workshops on the interests that the teens in your community already possess. The library can serve to connect teens to a successful future that they may not have known was possible.

If teens have a passion, it is never too early to start building that passion into skills they will need when entering a specific career field. We can help teens to locate options for acquiring these needed skills, from locating scholarships to take community college classes during the summer months to finding them articles, books, podcasts, or even internship opportunities related to a field of interest. We can also help teens discover previously unknown passions through hands-on workshops. As library staff, this is one way we can help teens progress towards becoming successful and fulfilled adults.

Notes

1. "Informational Interviewing," University of California Berkeley Career Center, https://career.berkeley.edu/Info/InfoInterview.
2. Sierra Tishgart, "Why You Need a Career Mentor and How to Find One," *Teen Vogue*, November 21, 2012, www.teenvogue.com/story/how-to-find-career -mentor.

5

Internships at the Library

REGARDLESS OF THE CAREERS TEENS PLAN TO PUR-sue, an internship can provide more than a handful of benefits to help them on their way. While pursuing a degree in creative writing in college, Amy was on the board of her school's literary journal and enjoyed the experience. She thought that working for a literary journal or magazine as a staff writer or editor would be a great career. She came up with the idea to seek out internships at a magazine—she was then living in New York City, so she had several options. A few months later, she took an unpaid internship at a design and fashion magazine that was one of her favorites. She was feeling great about this internship when she was selected and thought this was likely her key to entering the world of magazine publishing. However, it did not take her long to realize that the actual tasks required of the staff writers, editors, and designers did not appeal to her. Furthermore, the staff were mostly standoffish, unenthusiastic, and unhappy at work. She was thrilled when the four-month internship period was over—and did not apply for a second term although she was encouraged to stay. If she had not taken this internship, how else would she have known what it would be like to be employed by a magazine?

In contrast, like many of those reading this book, Amy pursued an internship while in an MLS program that was a wonderful experience that helped her obtain necessary skills and experience to land her first job after graduating. Without that internship, she would not have been hired right after graduation. Internships not only allow teens and young adults to test out career fields they are interested in, but also provide invaluable experience as well as skill-building and networking opportunities. There are numerous options available for internships in many career fields.

In this chapter, we will focus on a variety of internships in libraries across the United States. The internships described in this chapter not only allow teens to learn about libraries, but often focus on skills that may relate directly to other career fields. For example, some of the internships in this chapter allow teens to learn skills related to the fields of computer science, art, communication, and education. We sought to feature a broad variety of internship programs at a variety of libraries large and small with the hope that this information could help a library staff member who might be interested in creating an internship program. This chapter will also provide a variety of ideas that can help library staff improve an internship or volunteer program to increase its benefits to the teens participating.

BENEFITS OF INTERNSHIPS FOR TEENS AND YOUNG ADULTS

There are many benefits for teens who pursue an internship. Below, we list just a few that are usually takeaways from all internships, regardless of the field.

Internships help teens gain real-world knowledge of a field of interest. Even teens who take the time to research a career using books or online resources cannot obtain a deep understanding of what it is truly like to work in the field unless they have a chance to experience it for themselves. Take, for example, a teen who is interested in pursuing architecture. Her school counselor suggests an internship and the teen agrees. Of course, not every architecture firm is exactly alike; however, the internship will help this teen understand some of the daily tasks, challenges, and rewards she can expect when working at an architecture firm. She will gain an understanding of the skills that architects must have and some insight into whether these skills will be enjoyable to cultivate or might be a struggle. How successful did the teen feel about completing the tasks of the internship after receiving some training? This could provide some insight into what a future career in this area might be like. An internship is a low-commitment way to test out a career.

Internships help teens understand how to operate in a structured work environment. To maintain any job in the future, teens will need some basic skills. These skills include things like arriving at work on time, following basic procedures and policies, dressing appropriately for office environments, communicating clearly and respectfully with coworkers and perhaps customers, clients, or patrons; meeting deadlines or completing tasks on time, as well as a whole list of other transferable skills. Many internships also require interviews before an applicant is accepted, which may be a new experience for some teens. An internship experience will require teens to act professionally in ways that might not be expected of them in other areas of their lives.

Internships help teens determine which skills are needed to be successful in a specific field. Internships provide young people with a real-world look at the skills that are used each day by the professionals working in that field. Using the example of the architect again, architects must possess technical skills required for drafting building plans, but they also are likely to need skills to communicate clearly to clients or coworkers in meetings, e-mails, or reports. They may need to learn how to network, to conduct small talk, be approachable, and to practice a number of other skills that teens may not have considered when thinking about architecture. Teens can determine from internships if they already possess the required skills or if they will have to acquire them. Will these be a challenge for them or will they just require more practice?

Internships allow teens to network and make connections in the field. In some career fields who you know is essential to landing a great job. Internships are a way for young people to get to know successful people in their fields of interest. Furthermore, if a young person performs exceptionally during his internship, those professionals they have met may go out of their way to help this young person navigate a tricky job market. An intern should always make sure to leave a great impression, because you never know what that paid or unpaid internship might lead to—sometimes this may mean the organization that hosts an internship offers a permanent job at the end of the internship or after graduation.

Internships look great on a resume. Some career fields are difficult to break into as a newbie; an internship can make all the difference because it shows an employer that the applicant not only has some experience in a certain field, but also because pursuing an internship shows employers that an applicant is motivated and highly interested in the field. An internship can be an important first step towards a full-time, lucrative job.

Quality internships will improve a teen's confidence. A well-designed internship program will help teens capitalize on their existing skills and gain new ones in a supportive and encouraging environment. There should be training for interns as well as constructive feedback that helps them progress. Interns should be able to try out several different tasks during their internships, rather than being asked to complete only one task throughout their time with the organization; this will allow young people to obtain a well-rounded view of the career.

BENEFITS OF INTERNSHIPS FOR THE LIBRARY

Maybe your library has been considering starting an internship program for some time but you are not sure if you have enough time to maintain one. Starting an internship program should require discussion with a variety of staff members at your library. The program will indeed require work from staff—marketing, interviewing, training, providing feedback, showing appreciation, and other tasks that are essential to sustaining a successful internship program in a library setting. However, also consider the benefits to your library that running an internship program can reap.

Giving back to the community and supporting students. Internships are a perfect way to provide opportunities to youth in your community. An internship could be the first step to leading them on the path to a successful career. Libraries want to support those in our community and this is a concrete way to put our beliefs into action.

Investing in future library employees. Hosting an internship program is a terrific way to give back to the entire library community. Library job listings often ask for prior experience in a public library, but how are applicants able to gain that experience in the first place? A paid or unpaid internship is a terrific opportunity for someone interested in a career in libraries, an MLS student, or a recent graduate to gain the experience needed to land that first professional library position. Whether an intern eventually chooses to work at your library system or at another in the future, internships support the field of librarianship. If you do have an open position towards the end of the internship, it sometimes works out so that you could have a terrific new employee to hire who already knows a lot about your library's culture and goals.

Trained interns contribute to the workflow of the library. It is true that initially training an intern will take staff time and effort that decreases staff availability for regular tasks. However, once interns are trained, they provide hours of assistance to library staff, including completing tasks such as program preparation, program assistance, training volunteers, creating flyers or helping to market programs in other ways, assisting with the maintenance of the summer reading program, hosting pop-up programs, and other tasks that will free up library staff to concentrate on larger projects or planning. Interns generally take anywhere from a few days to a few weeks to train, depending on the types of tasks included in their internship. They then often give back several months of time to the library and usually contribute their best efforts because they know this is an opportunity that will help them prepare for their future goals.

Creating library advocates. Library interns and volunteers of all types will obtain a deep understanding of how your library system functions and all the work that goes into serving your community's needs. They often become loyal library advocates who help educate others about the amazing work that takes place because of all those hours of staff effort. This advocacy could be formal, such as speaking at a city council meeting in support of a new budget, or informally, by letting friends and family know about upcoming programs or just sharing about their enjoyable experiences while volunteering. When we create worthwhile and rewarding volunteer opportunities for community members, they reward us not only with the work they put in during their shifts, but also through their love of our library for many years to come. Invariably, this raises staff morale as well.

Adding new skills and interests that can be harnessed to improve what your library offers. Interns will likely bring skills and interests with them that vary from those of the staff employed at your library. Although interns may only be on the scene temporarily, they may contribute to instituting new changes that last beyond their internships. For example, your staff may not feel initially comfortable with coding, but when an intern suggests a coding program series for preteens, that can quickly change. The intern might plan the first workshop and host it with a staff member at the library. Staff members have the benefit of learning from the intern while increasing their comfort level with new technology. The workshop series might continue beyond this intern's time at the library, but it would never have come to fruition without their initiative. Interns are often high school, college, or graduate students, which means they are likely younger than many of the librarians. They may be ethnically, racially, or socioeconomically different from the librarians at your library. Interns should be encouraged to make suggestions and test out new ideas because these are ways for your library to stay relevant and tuned in to the needs of your community.

Opportunities for staff to develop skills to manage an internship program. An internship program is an opportunity to develop staff within your library. Managing a program requires that staff members meet deadlines, interview and hire interns, provide training and constructive feedback, and a whole list of other skill-building opportunities for the staff member in charge. Staff members who may want to become supervisors one day can gain management skills and insight. It will help staff increase their awareness of their strengths and identify opportunities for growth. If they struggled with giving directions to an intern, perhaps they need to work on their communication skills and provide directions in writing or demonstrate a task to the intern, rather than only giving verbal directions. If they are avoiding talking to an intern about a project that did not turn out as well as expected, they may find they are shying away from confrontation and must work to develop skills to constructively provide feedback to others.

HOW TO BEGIN PLANNING AN INTERNSHIP PROGRAM AT YOUR LIBRARY

As we have mentioned, running an internship program at your library can require increased work, especially in the stages when the program is being built from scratch. There are certainly many factors to consider before beginning an internship program. The list below contains questions that will help you tackle some of the potential issues from the get-go. If you can answer the questions below, you are on the way to building a plan for running a successful internship program at your library. In addition, if you are looking to propose a program to your manager or library director, having answers to these questions will help you to thoughtfully pitch the program.

- Who will oversee the program? (It is often beneficial to involve multiple staff members.)
- Who will create the policies and procedures for the program?
- How long will each session of the program last?
- Can interns reapply for another session?
- Will the internship program be offered throughout the year or will

your library only offer it during certain times of the year, such as spring or summer?

- Are there tasks that should not be completed by an intern? What are these tasks?
- What are the tasks you have available for intern's to complete and are these meaningful tasks that will ensure they have a high-quality internship experience?
- Who will train an intern?
- Do staff on your team have the capacity and enthusiasm to take on this project?
- Who is responsible for providing feedback to an intern, or terminating an internship if needed?
- How will the program be marketed to the community?
- Will this internship be paid or unpaid?
- How will you select applicants for the program?

Interns who have applied to the program and show an interest in libraries are generally going to do a terrific job. However, there are of course issues that could arise during an internship. That is why it is important to make sure staff at your library know their roles in working with an intern and why you must ask staff to provide the intern with regular constructive feedback to help them grow.

It is especially important to make sure interns work on meaningful tasks and that there is plenty of work to keep them involved. Busy work or unoccupied time will likely make interns feel like they are not being valued or as if they are wasting their time. In our experience, it makes all the difference to get to know the individual interns and learn about their interests. If you can match their interests with related tasks, they are more likely to enjoy their internships and be successful. We also always provide praise and thank them when they leave each day. Interns have been a very important part of the services we are able to provide to our community and we are grateful for their time with us.

We interviewed colleagues from libraries across the United States about their experiences with internship programs to provide you with additional ideas and tips.

High School Internship Program at Florida's Alachua County Library

An Interview with Erin Phemester, Senior Library Manager, Youth Services Department, Headquarters Branch of Alachua County Library District

Please briefly describe the internship program you offer for teens.

The Alachua County Library District strives to be a key to building a better community by creating opportunities to participate, connect, and discover. Our High School Internship program helps us to fulfill this mission by giving high school students in their junior or senior years an opportunity to discover library-related careers through hands-on participation. The goal of the program is to give teens a chance to learn what it is like to work in a library setting. The internship program is treated like any other job and requires applications, references, interviews, and job expectations.

The program is run three times during a fiscal year. Once in the fall, from late October through early December, once in spring from mid-February through mid-April, and once in the summer from mid-June through mid-August. These paid internships run nine weeks and students work ten hours per week. Following their orientation, they spend all their time at their assigned location.

Explain the benefits you hope teens receive from participating in this program.

No matter where teens are placed, we hope that they get the same basic benefits from the internship program. We want them to learn job skills such as customer service, basic e-mail use, effective communication skills, and time management. To help them learn these skills, interns receive a staff mentor at their location. These staff members help supervise and train the interns. They also set the interns' schedules to meet the needs of the branch or department. They provide one-on-one mentorship to help teens learn basic library tasks like shelving, checking patrons in or out, providing readers' advisory, or programming support. Some mentors help teens generate a resume during their internship as a way to introduce them to the Library eSources. One eSource has a resume template and patrons frequently ask for help with the forms. This also allows teens to walk away from the internship with a completed resume.

How do you market the program to teens in the community?
Teens are invited to participate in the program via their high school guidance office, library district social media, library district website, or word of mouth from staff and former participants.

How are teens selected for the internship program?
Once they decide to apply, teens must complete an application packet and have all materials turned in by the deadline. The application packet consists of:

- an application form
- a personal essay answering the question "what do you hope to gain from your experience in the ACLD High School Internship program?"
- a letter of recommendation from a teacher of their choosing, or, in the case of homeschool students, an adult outside of their family who can speak to their abilities
- a parent/legal guardian release form
- high school transcripts

Applicants are then invited for an interview with staff at the branch or department where they are interested in working. Questions include, "why are you interested in this internship?" "what is your previous experience with libraries including your time as a patron?" and "tell us about previous job or volunteer experience." These questions are designed to help teens understand the interview process and think about how their life experience can qualify them for entry-level jobs. Selected teens are then sent for a drug screen.

Following the application process, selected teens participate in an orientation where they receive an explanation of job expectations. For many teens, this is the first time they learn about following a schedule, how to call in if they have an emergency, and juggling priorities when it comes to school, extracurricular activities, and work. Teens also receive instruction on how to sign up for payroll. Teens are then told when to report to their assigned locations. Each location has different tasks and instructions for the teens. Some teens work in circulation and learn the entire process of getting a book from the shelf to the patron and checking it back in. Other teens go to outreach services and learn about taking out the bookmobiles, delivering materials throughout the district, and sorting interlibrary loan deliveries. Still other teens get the benefit of being in a branch and experiencing all aspects of branch life from circulation to programming to community involvement.

Do you offer any other workforce-development opportunities to the teens in this program?

Staff mentors are not the only ones who help interns during their time at the library district. Other staff enjoy helping interns learn more about their departments or branches and the library district as a whole.

Do you have any quotes from teen participants that you could share with us?

One former intern, Bridget, said that she "enjoyed being a part of the Circulation Department. Everyone was very nice and helpful." Maybe that's why Bridget decided to apply for a regular position with the library district after her internship. In fact, we have many high school interns who go on to apply for page positions following their internships. This is a benefit to us as well as them. It is great to have a new employee who is already familiar with how the library district operates.

At the end of the internship program, interns and their mentors have a closing party to talk about what they learned in their internships, what they enjoyed, and what they would tell someone considering the internship program. Former intern Desiree said, "I highly encourage people to participate in the internship program. It was a lot of fun, it prepares you for a real job, it helps you to understand how complex the library is, and it was a great way to meet my community."

Is there anything else you would like to tell us about this program?

We are very proud of our internship program and we love when we have interns apply for positions after their internships are completed. Many interns have returned to the library district and have worked their way up to full-time positions. Some of them have even served as mentors to new high school interns. Internship programs are a great way to help teens and the community at large understand the diverse job skills and job duties that are housed in the library. Teens are always surprised to learn about the variety of internship locations open to them. If you are considering an internship program at your location, we highly encourage you to take that leap and start a program. We would be happy to answer any questions you might have regarding our internship program.

Community Learning Internships at Kitsap Regional Library

An Interview with Megan Burton, Teen Services Librarian, Kitsap Regional Library, Washington

Please briefly describe the internship program you offer for teens.

We provide rolling 100-hour paid Community Learning internships to youth ages 16 to 25 at each of our nine county locations. Youth are asked to leverage personal interests to create a project that supports our STEM learning initiative. These projects are as varied as the youth that we work with and have ranged from tutorials for youth and library staff on specific technologies to needs assessments, program co-design and implementation, etc.

Explain the benefits you hope teens receive from participating in this program.

Our goal is to provide teens with an opportunity to build twenty-first-century college- and career-readiness skills in a low-stakes environment. Because of this process, we are able to meaningfully integrate youth voices into our efforts and therefore create more community-driven, authentic work.

Do you offer any other workforce-development opportunities to the teens in this program?

Providing coaching during the application and interview process has been a priority and something that we'd like to further strengthen. This is probably not true in 100 percent of our internships, but supporting youth in a mentoring capacity beyond the "official" internship has certainly been a practice that our staff have embraced. I've really enjoyed hearing about what our former interns have gone on to do and the love that they've shared for us in playing a part to get them there. Appreciation for "my KRL family" has been included in at least two updates that I've received from staff.

During the final phase of their work, we ask staff and interns to discuss what they learned and how they can express that in a way that's meaningful to them. We offer digital badges, but some take these ideas to college applications, LinkedIn, or resumes. As a specific example, we hired one of our pilot interns to serve in a permanent peer-mentor position. She was so creative and open to problem-solving, we knew that with her firsthand knowledge or the program, she'd be a great asset to other youth.

How do you market the program to teens in the community?
This program is marketed heavily though word of mouth and through our local partners (county agencies, school counselors, youth organizations, etc.). We also can post via our community college.

How are teens selected for the internship program?
Teens go through a formal application and interview process. Our goal is to provide as many youths as we can with that learning opportunity. From there, our librarians are given the freedom to decide which youth best fits the current needs of the library. Our priority is to work with youth with high barriers first, but issues like capacity or schedule conflicts are also taken into consideration in making final decisions.

Is there anything else you would like to tell us about this program?
Our intern program is one of the most labor-intensive initiatives that our librarians work on but easily one of the most successful in terms of impact, both for the individual as well as for staff and the organization. We've learned so much through this process and it's truly opened the eyes of everyone in our organization about the role that we/they can play in supporting and leveraging the voices of youth in our community.

Service Learning at Seattle Public Library

An Interview with Josie Watanabe, Youth and Family Learning Team, Seattle Public Library

Please briefly describe the internship program you offer for teens.
Service learning at The Seattle Public Library connects classroom and community to real issues and meets community needs through collaborative learning and building community leaders; seeks to benefit both the provider and recipient of service; and focuses equally on the service being performed, skills acquired, and learning that is occurring.

A successful service learning program must have high warmth, high expectations, and high structure.

1. *High warmth:* Teens feel welcome and safe. Always attend to their emotional, social, and physical needs.

2. *High expectations:* Communicate high and clear expectations to the teens. Then create structure to help teens meet the expectations.

3. *High structure:* Service learning activities must be responsive to the needs of the library and the community (not just based on the teens' dreams and desires). Structure will enable teens to have clear boundaries for developing their projects. A set schedule and predictable components for service learning meetings will help provide program structure.

Three Components of the Library's Service Learning Projects:

1. *Projects must be teen driven:* We would like the projects that teens are working on to be aligned with their interests and passions. Teen voices will guide the development, planning, implementation, and reflection phases of projects.

2. *Projects must meet a community need:* Is the community interested in the product of the project? How can teens determine if a project meets a need in the community?

3. *Projects must meet a need at the library:* Is the teens' project aligned with one of the Library's service priorities?

Explain the benefits you hope teens receive from participating in this program.

Teens will be able to practice their project management, leadership, and collaborative skills while planning projects that meet a community and/or library need.

Do you offer any other workforce-development opportunities to the teens in this program?

The program is tied to workforce-development skills and so resume, mentoring, and other internship opportunities could be on a teen's action plan. It's a teen-driven program and so the teens decide if they want that type of assistance. The library also offers other programs on finding a job, resume skills, and a workshop on how to apply to be a library student assistant.

How do you market the program to teens in the community?

We rely on community engagement between the librarians, community organizations, and schools. At each library the service learning programs are small, between five to eight teens, so that the librarians can give the group the attention and support it needs to develop a program or project. The programs/projects are marketed by the teen service learners.

How are teens selected for the internship program?
We conducted a survey of teen opportunities in the city before we started this program and found there were many programs for high achieving teens and at-risk teens, but very few for the "neighborhood teen." Neighborhood teens may not have parents who are driving them to their extracurricular activities or can check over a resume or job application. This program was designed to develop college and career skills for the "neighborhood teen." We have interested teens fill out an application and go through an interview for the job skill experience. The goal of each program is to get a group of six to eight teens who have a variety of abilities, skill levels, and interests.

Do you have any quotes from teen participants that you could share with us?
When the planned Artists in Action series had only one attendee, service learners worked on presenting an additional event on a Friday and decided on a different marketing and publicity plan to see if they could boost attendance. One teen showed impressive leadership and motivational skills as well as his appreciation for the library and the service-learning experience. The teen commented to Cheresse, "To be perfectly honest, I was very surprised myself. It's actually a side of me that I've never ever seen or experienced before, but the motivation to do better in the second semester is what drove me to strive. The motivation of experiencing teen programs won't allow me to give up on this one no matter how much of a bad idea I thought it was or anyone thought it was. I have high spirits along with [Teen 2] and [Teen 3] and we're all determined to make this work together! I told them both they have the option to opt out of the program if they want, but I was going to stay and make it work regardless how I manage to do it but they both said they'd stay and the three of us are going to make one hell of an art festival come March 11th, you have my word on that!"

Is there anything else you would like to tell us about this program?
This program has helped move teen-serving librarians from "experts" to facil-

itators and has changed the way they work with teens. They are no longer creating programs based on what they think teens want or need, but instead helping teens to create programs for their community, based on community need.

T4 at Brooklyn Public Library

An Interview with Jackson Gomes, T4 Project Coordinator, Brooklyn Public Library

Please briefly describe the internship program you offer for teens.
Today's Teens, Tomorrow's Techies (T4) is a volunteer program in which teens, ages 14 through 18, receive free technology training as preparation for collaborating with Brooklyn Public Library staff to enhance the library's service to the public. The T4s serve by teaching, mentoring, and sharing knowledge with staff and patrons. Currently in its thirteenth year of operation, the program has engaged more than 1,500 teens to date. Every summer the program accepts eighty applicants for participation in a mandatory two-week training period. The T4 Summer Technology Institute comprises eight four-hour workshops, totaling thirty-two hours of training. Its curriculum is primarily based in Microsoft Office programs such as Excel, PowerPoint, and Word; customer service; and library technology.

Upon completion of their Summer Institute Training, T4s are placed in one of Brooklyn Public Library's fifty-eight locations. They are required to participate in 120 hours of community service at their location over the course of the school year. Of these, twenty hours consist of elective workshops and field trips to colleges, universities, museums, and businesses to expand their awareness of what a future in technology could bring. These school-year elective workshops provide training in more advanced programs and coding languages. Electives include training such as Adobe Photoshop, Adobe Dreamweaver, Adobe Illustrator, 3-D printing, hardware upgrade and repair, littleBits, and Lego Robotics. As part of the electives, T4s participate in chat sessions with professionals in the technology field. They also participate in an Animation/Comic Book Club where they read selected comic books and graphic novels and hold group discussions. As part of the Animation/Comic Book Club final project, participants design their own digital comics and learn to create animation. In the robotics club, T4s can experiment with electronics and provide a forum for discussion and sharing information. Participation in this club enhances their knowledge of engineering, science, programming, mathematics, problem-solving, project design, and management. Using Lego Mindstorm EV3 Robots, students are given the knowledge and hands-on experience to assemble and program their own creations.

T4s' responsibilities in the branches included assisting technology resource specialists (TRS) by troubleshooting more advanced technology problems, and applying skills learned in training workshops. All T4s are trained and equipped to assist TRS and librarian staff in delivering computer training programs to the public. During the school year all T4s provide free computer training classes to other teens, adults, seniors, and kids in their neighborhood libraries.

Explain the benefits you hope teens receive from participating in this program.

- free tech skills training that will help them build a strong resume
- customer service skills that help them with employment opportunities in the future
- encouragement to learn more about information technology careers and opportunities that are out there for young people
- teaching our teens to be leaders in their community
- skills that will help with the competitive world they live in

Do you offer any other workforce-development opportunities to the teens in this program?

Our program is based on a mentor/mentee relationship. All T4s have a mentor at the library that they shadow and learn how to help patrons with tech-related questions. The T4s always comment in their final reflective essays how much they enjoy working with the mentor at their designated library. Many of them after graduating ask their mentor for recommendation letters or job references. They stay in contact long after. Some are lucky enough that their mentor helps them find a part-time job opportunity at Brooklyn Public Library.

All the T4s create their resumes during the summer institute curriculum. As they go through the program, they update their resumes to reflect the various tech training they receive through the program. We also expose them to our databases, which introduces them to career cruising and helps them to formulate ideas about careers in the tech field. During their forums (graduation events), tech professionals (web designers, computer engineers, game designers, programmer etc.) present about their career paths and talk to them about their field of work. It is also an opportunity for them to network with professionals.

How do you market the program to teens in the community?

- We do a massive recruitment by sending newsletters to all high schools in the boroughs of New York City.
- We use our promotional video on our website.
- We have flyers in all fifty-eight library locations.
- Library staff and I do outreach in schools.
- Word-of-mouth—many of our graduates recommend their friends and family to apply.

How are teens selected for the internship program?
We hold interview sessions from April to June. We look for teens who wish to give back to their communities and envision the benefit of gaining exposure to tech training that will help them learn more about the information technology job field.

Do you have any quotes from teen participants that you could share with us?

I was given the opportunity to explore coding, robotics, game design, and test my skills in new areas. I love to learn, and the T4 program expanded my horizons to the things that I thought weren't immediately available to me. —*Kemba*

Albert Einstein once said, "The only source of knowledge is experience." As I finish my hours at the library, not only has my knowledge of computers broadened, but I had an opportunity to work with the most wonderful people in my community. —*Christine*

My interest in technology and the STEM field in general was definitely bolstered through this amazing experience. —*Arvin*

After teaching her, I felt a sense of fulfillment and purpose because I was able to give someone the ability to perform such a useful and basic life skill. At that moment I understood why being a T4 was so important. Beyond helping people do something in a single moment, I can give them a skill that they will use for the rest of their life. —*Julian*

Is there anything else you would like to tell us about this program?
Over the years we have been lucky that our graduates continue to return to Brooklyn Public Library to volunteer in other capacities (homework helper, shelf organizer, etc.). We have also been fortunate to receive funding to run a Summer Ambassador program in which T4 alum have returned to Brooklyn Public Library for the summer and assisted with summer reading programs and tech programs for the public. Our tech teachers have years of teaching experience. One is an MIT engineering graduate; another is a tech professor at Pace University. Many of our T4 graduates have had the opportunity to be hired by Brooklyn Public Library. One of our employees who is a network support representative was originally a T4. We also have a young adult librarian that was originally a T4.

Summer and Spring Internships at Beaverton City Library

An Interview with Jennifer Johnson, Manager of Volunteer Services, Beaverton City Library, Beaverton, Oregon

Please briefly describe the internship program you offer for teens/young adults.
For more than a decade, the Beaverton City Library has been a local leader in providing teaching internships and practicums for students. We provide experiences working directly with patrons, supervising teen volunteers, leading programs, and more. Successful candidates will have the option to select three additional learning opportunities within the division for which they are interning and/or another area of the library. Interns gain professional experience in library youth services during our busy summer season. They will

also gain leadership skills as they help coordinate the work of approximately forty teen volunteers. We strive to make our internships teaching internships—offering interns the opportunity to learn about reference, collection development, and program planning. Volunteer internships are generally ten to twelve weeks in length with interns contributing ten to twenty hours per week. We encourage library school, undergraduate, and high school students to apply.

Explain the benefits you hope teens receive from participating in this program.

Our internship and practicum opportunities are unpaid, but the benefits are *amazing!* As an intern at the Beaverton City Library, you will gain valuable professional skills, build your resume with meaningful work, earn a letter of recommendation and *have fun!*

Do you offer any other workforce-development opportunities to the teens in this program?

We do offer job shadowing. Also, many former interns stick around and continue developing work relationships with library staff. This has included finding new, meaningful volunteer assignments, assisting with resumes, writing letters and recommendations long after their internships, and more. I have been invited and attended several high school graduation ceremonies, too!

How do you market the program to teens in the community?

I send our internship openings to all active and some inactive volunteers entering the junior or senior year of high school. I also send it to a select group of students who will be entering sophomore year—if they have been volunteering for a while and seem to have a good work ethic, they make the cut. We also have information available on our website about internships mentioning possibilities for teens. Also, during their initial volunteer interview with me the possibility of internships might come up in conversation and I let them know that I hope they explore an internship opportunity.

How are teens selected for the internship program?

All internship applicants need to complete a volunteer application and send a resume and cover letter. All applicants are interviewed by me (the volunteer manager) and the supervising division manager. Top applicants are chosen.

Do you have any quotes from teen participants that you could share with us?

> My internship experience was amazing! I really enjoyed working with the staff and volunteers and learned so much from everyone. Thank you for giving me this opportunity. —*Intern, age 18*

> The most helpful thing I learned was to go for it. I learned that I should have confidence when contributing, put my best foot forward, and really put some personality into my work. —*Intern, age 16*

Is there anything else you would like to tell us about this program?
Without a teen intern, I would not have been able to move forward with our volunteer database back in 2010. A very smart, hard-working, lovely student transferred data, set permissions, made edits, and slogged through stacks of paperwork and endless changes from me. She created the framework for our use of Volgistics and I could not have done or imagined it without her. I often referred to her as the smartest teenager I knew. She was sixteen years old. And amazing. And we are still in touch with each other.

Teen Interns at Silver City Public Library

An Interview with Chris Baumgarn, Youth Services Librarian, Silver City Public Library, Silver City, New Mexico

Please briefly describe the internship program you offer for teens.
We currently have teen volunteers, and also have had teen volunteers in the past, but this is the first year that we had a teen internship program at our library. Our intern was paid $1,000 for completing the program, which was funded by our library board. It was just for the summer but worked out so well we are planning to do it again next summer. Perhaps if the success continues our board might consider employing a teen intern during the school year as well. Our teen intern this year worked, on average, sixteen hours a week for eight weeks. This constituted the duration of our summer reading program. She helped with typical things such as shelving, making popcorn, and setting up for programs. I also gave her a major project to do over the

summer for when she had free time, which was to go through all the book series in the children's collection to see what our library is missing. This was a large and ambitious project and for the most part our intern did not have time to concentrate on it, so she was only able to get to a few shelves during her time here. The intern was also very helpful with mentoring our kids of all ages as they worked on projects throughout the summer. The intern also took pictures of all our activities throughout the summer and then put together a video to show at our end of the summer party.

Explain the benefits you hope teens receive from participating in this program.

In the town we live in, Silver City, opportunities for teens to work are very minimal. By providing this internship we were hoping to give a teenage person the opportunity to see what it is like working in a small public library and providing services to his or her community. First off, we hope she was able to have fun with the programs we provided over the summer and give us feedback if we were doing anything that teens her age might not be interested in. Working over the summer meant having to sacrifice her free time and developing the discipline to stick to a schedule when many of her friends were sleeping in or just having fun. She needed to collaborate with the rest of the library's employees to get the work done properly and be able to communicate with the public, both children and parents. We hope that this opportunity with our library will be something she can put on her college resume as well as help her as she starts into her first job. And on top of everything else, hopefully this experience helped her to develop an appreciation and love for public libraries.

How do you market the program to teens in the community?

We did list this position in the newspaper but did not get any results from that platform. The results we did get were from going through high school counselors and advertising in the schools.

How are teens selected for the internship program?

Teens had to be at least sixteen years of age to satisfy the town's requirements. We conducted interviews for everyone who applied. I was impressed by all the candidates but the intern we chose had the advantage of having volunteered in a public library in the past.

Is there anything else you would like to tell us about this program?

I think it is important for teens doing a program like this not to be just shelving or shelf-reading all summer. They should have the opportunity to show off their personalities to the public. They should also be part of the decision-making process when possible and take part in evaluating the program at the end of the summer.

VolunTeen Program at Charlotte Mecklenburg Library

An Interview with Kelly N. Czarnecki, Loft Manager, ImaginOn, Charlotte Mecklenburg Library, North Carolina

Please briefly describe the internship program you offer for teens.

Throughout our twenty locations, including ImaginOn, we offer the year-round unpaid VolunTeen program for teens where applications are accepted three times a year. This workforce-development initiative gives teens the opportunity to gain job experiences by having a schedule, learning more about the library through helping shelve materials or develop programs, and grow their leadership. Several branches in the system also offer the Satellite Studios internship. This gives teens the chance to teach customers how to use digital media including animation, blue screen technology, and music creation. Although ImaginOn doesn't have a Satellite Studios internship, we do have Studio i, which also utilizes similar digital media and is a kind of makerspace and is part of the VolunTeen program responsibilities. It's only within the last five years that Studio i hasn't existed as a stand-alone internship. With makerspaces becoming more commonplace in libraries, and Studio i a core service that we offer, it was a more natural fit to be folded into the VolunTeen program itself.

We structure the program to be interest-driven. This means that some teens may gravitate more toward working with their peers in Studio i while others enjoy being with younger visitors through other programming such as science experiments. Although they all get a chance to do general tasks such as shelving or pulling holds, they may find themselves more concentrated in one area over another. These are organized as "tracks" for the VolunTeens with basic skills defined and then leveling up once they've shown proficiency. This is also a great way for teens that return to increase their skills and vary their experiences.

Explain the benefits you hope teens receive from participating in this program.

Through the VolunTeen program, teens are able to develop their interests and knowledge of the library. They are in a supportive environment so if they do need to improve job skills such as communicating if absent or need more information about a particular task, they are reminded to do so and typically progress over time and can take these skills to their next experiences. They often will develop those "soft skills" such as being more comfortable talking and interacting with a variety of people whether it be peers or adults. Every teen that applies and goes through the program doesn't have the same end goal, of course. We hope the benefits the teens receive meet them where they are —whether it be to build social skills, time management, responsibility, or work experience.

Do you offer any other workforce-development opportunities to the teens in this program?

We've been trying new strategies with the program the past few years. One example was that those who were interviewed for the position but didn't get accepted were given the opportunity to improve their interviewing skills through relevant workshops such as mock interviewing or resume building. Another is that we have community service programs throughout the year. If applicants don't get the volunteer position they interviewed for but are still seeking hours, they can attend a service program at a branch and achieve their goal that way. The program could be anything from making blankets for the Linus Project to 3-D printing prosthetic hands.

How do you market the program to teens in the community?

We utilize pretty typical ways of marketing—through word of mouth; the library website and more specifically the teen page: www.cmlibrary.org/services/teen-services; and social media including Facebook, Twitter, and Instagram. We'll post flyers in our branches and share them with community organizations including schools.

How are teens selected for the internship program?

There is an application period and interview process. Because we receive more applications than we have positions for, teens are selected using a variety of criteria. For example, if they are returning from a previous term and have demonstrated strong skills, they will likely remain in the program. Though to be open to new teens we try to keep a balance of those returning and those wanting to enter the program. Other criteria may include availability during the term. If they are planning on having several vacations or aren't able to work the hours we need, it would be best if they reapply at another time. If the teens themselves wouldn't express much interest in the position if it weren't for their parents, that can also be an indication that they might not be ready at this time to participate. These are some of the factors that are taken into consideration to select teens into the program.

Do you have any quotes from teen participants that you could share with us?
We have quotes from teens when the Studio i Internship program existed:

> This is a great learning experience and I have come to love this place. The technologies I learned have helped me with many school projects that astounded my teachers. It also feels great to volunteer my time in helping others rather than to sit around my home and lazily watch TV. I would recommend this internship program to my peers because Studio i not only teaches a person technology skills, but also communication and leadership skills. It has helped me grow as a person.

> My good friend Treena, a current intern, told me about this internship and it has been such a great experience. I've learned and grown as a person and this internship emphasized my dream to be a part of the filmmaking industry one day. I have recommended this internship to my peers because it makes people better people.

> I would recommend the Studio i internship program to my peers because I feel that going through this program has helped me overall become a better person. I feel like I accomplished my goal by giving time to my community by helping kids with projects.

> I would recommend this program to a friend, because I really received a hands-on experience. Studio i is a "playground" for anyone into animation, music and film. It was a very interesting and fun internship.

Is there anything else you would like to tell us about this program?
The VolunTeen program aims to give teens a meaningful experience. We're always looking for and implementing ways to improve and grow the program. As teens' needs and skills change, we must remain relevant to continue building the abilities they need. One way we do this is through the Lead Volun-Teen position within the program. This is open to teens who have been in the program for at least a year and have demonstrated positive behaviors. They gain increased responsibility with the program including helping to mentor incoming VolunTeens. The leadership component of the program is helpful for them to include on their resume!

The Ground Floor at Monroe County Public Library

An Interview with Kevin MacDowell, Teen Services/Digital Creativity Strategist, Monroe County Public Library, Bloomington, Indiana

Please briefly describe the internship/volunteer programs you offer for teens.
At the Monroe County Public Library's new teen space, The Ground Floor, our patrons are given the opportunity to hang out, mess around, and geek out in a space that has many materials, resources, and programs that we believe lead to the acquisition of twenty-first century literacy skills and aid in teens' future readiness. Opportunities to build pro-social skills, cultural sensitivity, teamwork and collaboration skills, and relationships with caring adults are just the beginning of the assets that can be acquired through participating in our space. When taken in tandem with opportunities in our digital creativity center to learn digital media production and acquire those types of digital literacies, we feel that our regular patrons are absolutely being armed with skills and opportunities to allow for nontraditional career paths and future readiness.

Additionally, we do offer a volunteer opportunity for teens to learn how to set up and run two of our VR rigs, the Oculus Rift and the HTC Vive. Teens receive a two-hour training for this opportunity, then sign up for the rotation of scheduled VR programs we offer in the library. They come to these scheduled programs and nearly run the programs on their own, with a staff person present to assist only when needed or asked for.

In our most recent strategic planning process, our teen services and digital creativity unit identified that workforce development is an area that we need to further develop in the next three years and are therefore looking to develop a teen internship program. In this program, teens will be mentored by professional teen librarians and will assist in program planning, setup, and implementation. VR will continue to be an area of programming that will be included in these future endeavors, as well as upcoming 3-D printing programming.

Explain the benefits you hope teens receive from participating in this program.
We hope for teens to have as many varied experiences and opportunities as possible while they hang out, mess around, and geek out in our space, so that they might begin to develop a sense for what it is they love to do and then do more of that, thereby building a deeper skill set in that area. We hope that teens who volunteer in our VR programming will benefit from the training in setting up and running VR experiences so that they build deeper digital literacy. We also expect them to develop leadership skills, and pro-social behavior. Finally, we expect them to benefit from engaging with staff as adults who care about them and their future—a fundamental, and developmental asset in youth development.

Do you offer any other workforce-development opportunities to the teens in this program?
Not yet, but it is in our strategic development plan to pursue future readiness in depth in the next three years.

How do you market the program to teens in the community?
Right now, we only market volunteer opportunities to teens who already visit our teen space via face-to-face invitations and some social media posts. We market our space and the opportunities to hang out, mess around, and geek out (which we believe leads to the acquisition of twenty-first century literacy skills, thereby assisting in future readiness) via regular school visits throughout the year, social media posts, and via local media (e.g., radio, newspaper).

How are teens selected for the internship program?
Teens who indicate they want to be a part of the VR volunteer program sim-

ply need to show up to and complete the training. After that, they are put in rotation for scheduling.

Do you have any quotes from teen participants that you could share with us?

I might go into computer programming or something like it.

And the most valuable thing I've learned is how to set up VR equipment.

Is there anything else you would like to tell us about this program?
We look forward to further developing a teen internship program in the next three years as part of the action plan informed by our most recent strategic planning process.

HOW TO ENSURE YOUR INTERNSHIP PROGRAM IS SUSTAINABLE

Imagine your work could result in an internship program that runs for three or five or fifteen years at your library system. This might mean the program continues to function long after you may have moved on to another job or retired. Some of the case study libraries featured above have had long-running internship programs, but of course the programs have been refined and tweaked over the years. To begin a program that could run for many years at your library, it is very important to begin with staff buy-in. If most staff are on board with the program and enthusiastic to welcome new interns, this will hopefully prompt the culture to move forward over the years.

Clear procedures for the internship program will help garner staff buy-in and ensure a long-running program. Staff will want to know what is expected of them in relation to the interns, and the interns will need to know which staff to go to when they need help. Written procedures also ensure the program can be passed to another staff member without great issue.

Your library will also want to create a process for evaluating the internship program. This will include feedback provided to the interns at the conclusion of their time with the library, feedback from the interns about their experiences, as well as feedback from staff about the program and their involvement in it. All this input will help whoever is in charge of the program evaluate if any elements need to change moving forward. This feedback is imperative to making sure your program is sustainable because it helps avoid issues that may not have otherwise been apparent, allowing for a change in course for a future internship session if needed.

CONCLUSION

The examples of internship programs included in this chapter are meant to provide ideas and inspiration for internship programs at your library. As you have seen, there are a wide variety of options for setting up and facilitating an internship or volunteer program for teens and young adults. What these programs all have in common is that each of these unique programs yield benefits for the libraries hosting them and for the participants. What we observed from our interviews with librarians all over the country is the passion they have for working with the youth in these programs.

Starting a program from scratch can require a substantial investment of time; however, using some of the ideas from the case studies, as well as reaching out to other libraries that run programs like what you may be imagining, can help you take those first steps. Each internship or volunteer program will of course be unique to the specific library and the community that it serves. In our experience, all the work that goes into setting up an internship or volunteer program becomes manageable when you have a chance to witness the amazing benefits for the teens who participate.

6

The Fast Track:
Trade School Fair

N 2015, THREE LIBRARY STAFF MEMBERS IN THE LOFT FOUND themselves in an informal meeting, discussing how to introduce the teens they served to trade schools, vocational certificate programs, and historically black colleges. Our colleague Jimmeka was primarily interested in bringing together representatives from local historically black colleges to share information. She particularly wanted them to share information about any funding or scholarships their institutions might offer and describe the culture and support systems at their schools. Marie had recently learned about Mike Rowe's Profoundly Disconnected Foundation (http://profoundlydisconnected.com), which provides scholarships to students seeking opportunities for post-high school education or certification in vocational skills. By the end of our excited discussion, it was decided: we would combine the two ideas and provide the best of the best to our teens. We would host a fair at our library featuring representatives from local vocational schools and organizations that granted scholarships or financial aid to students who enrolled in these schools. In our excited daydreaming phase, we envisioned inviting Profoundly Disconnected staff (why not Mike Rowe himself?) to attend. (Spoiler alert: Mike Rowe did not come to our library branch.) Jimmeka began listing all the contacts we had developed through a previous program, including cosmetologists, hair stylists, barbers, photographers, and radio personalities. Amy was able to contribute the name of the nearest school offering a veterinary technician program and knew people who we could invite to speak on a panel. Marie hadn't yet developed contacts but was eager to begin researching and was not shy about reaching out to professionals and schools. Over the course of the next three months, we three library staffers worked hard to pull together a trade school fair from scratch—we had a vision and we pursued it enthusiastically. We e-mailed and called over a dozen trade schools in our area and contacted our state's college-funding organization. Marie refused to give up on Profoundly Disconnected and contacted its staff to see if they would at least provide print materials for distribution at the event. We hired a DJ to attract teens to the event and arranged for a panel discussion so that teens could hear about careers from professionals who were currently working in different vocations. As we contacted schools, we encouraged the representatives to bring hands-on activities, explaining that the primary audience would be teenagers, who are more likely to be engaged by physical examples. Although we had no prior experience hosting this type of event, our teamwork made it all possible. Undoubtedly, working together in the same department made communication easier than it would have been had we been scattered in separate buildings. We also shared a Google Sheet for planning and keeping track of information as it was gathered.

We are getting ahead of our narrative here. Let us back up to the very beginning: Why host a trade school fair? What started our conversation that day?

WHY HOST A TRADE SCHOOL FAIR?

Some librarians may ask why they should go to the trouble of planning and executing such a large program for their teen patrons. In the first chapter we discussed how both President Obama and the United States Department of Education called for technical and vocational skills training. We discussed the skills gap, or how there are more jobs than there are skilled workers to fill them. The National Skills Coalition estimates that 54 percent of jobs in America today fall into the category of "skilled work," but that only 44 percent of Americans have the necessary skills. We will also refer you back to figure 1.2, where you will see that the expected salaries in these middle-skills careers are certainly livable wages. In Charlotte, North Carolina, we recently saw a billboard advertising that there would be new jobs moving into the area, and therefore skilled laborers would be needed. (The billboard was advertising our county's community college.) This was followed by a news segment about how the skilled labor shortage in the area was driving up housing costs because of a lack of carpenters, plumbers, and electricians.[1]

Many groups of teens crave these types of educational programs and perform much better in them than in traditional schools. Perhaps no one else in their families has attended college, and they cannot picture themselves doing so either. Perhaps their families rely on their physical or financial assistance at home, and they must begin working as soon as possible after high school. Or perhaps they simply disliked high school immensely and do not want to pursue any further education beyond what is absolutely necessary. Whatever their reasons, there is a growing number of teens who simply are not ready for or interested in traditional four-year colleges and universities. However, it has been shown that students who pursue an associate's degree or comparable certificate program increase their lifetime earnings potential over those students who do not pursue further education post-high school.[2]

Teen-serving library staff can be instrumental in assisting teens with navigating through these choices. We are often placed in positions of informal (or formal) mentorship with the students that we serve, and we can help them to make informed decisions about which path is right for them. They may be feeling pressure from parents or teachers to look at four-year colleges but are not sure that is the right choice for them. Conversely, maybe no other adults in their lives are encouraging them to think about education past high school. We can present students with options and show them that there are advantages no matter what type of education they choose after high school. An event like the Fast Track: Trade School Fair can help bring together teens and vocational schools.

STEPS FOR PLANNING A TRADE SCHOOL FAIR AT YOUR LIBRARY

Once you have decided that you will host a trade school fair at your library, you will have to consider when and where to hold the event, who among your staff and colleagues to include, which institutions to invite, and what audience you hope will participate.

The timing of your event will most likely be specific to your branch's location and patron base. Within the Charlotte Mecklenburg Library system, two library branches currently hold annual vocational fairs, and they hold them in different months. When we worked with teens at ImaginOn, we knew that as a central location we should look at county-wide trends when planning our Fast Track program. There was a separate team of staff from other branches that planned a series of college-readiness programs for the system. The team had a helpful big-picture view of what similar programs were being offered for teens on various weekends. After checking with this team, we were able to select a weekend in March when no other competing college-readiness programs were offered. You may be wondering if there was a reason for selecting March, and there was: the college-readiness programming team advised us that many teens would be starting to take SATs and ACTs in February and beginning to tour and apply to colleges and universities in March or April. We, of course, wanted to hold our program at a time of year when after-high-school planning was forefront in teenagers' minds. We would offer a caveat here: the time of year when your teens are beginning to consider their post-high school plans may be different in your location. The other library branch in Charlotte that holds an annual vocational programs fair does so in May. It is a smaller branch, most of whose program attendees are teens in their immediate vicinity. In speaking with their teen regulars and with the nearby high school, the staff discovered that a variety of influences converge later in the spring to bring post-high school planning to the attention of their patrons. For your library branch, this might happen in the fall. To get information on the best time of year for this type of program, we recommend talking to your teen patrons. It may come up in conversation that they are starting to wonder about their next steps. Look to your community: when is the local college/university fair? If it is well-attended, you can use that as an indication that your community is aware of the need for post-high school planning at that time of year, and plan to hold your event on a weekend during the same month. (Do not, however, schedule your vocational school fair the same weekend as your community college/university fair. This is most likely commonsense advice, but you do not want to compete with a big local event.) For additional insight, you might consult with local high school guidance counselors and check the Princeton Review website to discover SAT and ACT testing dates.

We found it reassuring and helpful to work as a small team to plan and execute the event. In our inaugural year, we worked with our colleague Jimmeka, and in the second year we worked with our colleague Victoria. After the second annual Fast Track: Trade School Fair, both of us took on new positions that furthered our careers but took us away from the Teen Loft at

ImaginOn. Our history of including multiple team members in the planning and facilitation meant that the program did not end with our departure: Victoria was able to invite her colleague Paulina to assist with putting on the third annual Fast Track: Trade School Fair. We imagine that the fourth annual event will be taken on by Paulina and a new colleague or two. This method of event execution is not only applicable to vocational school fairs; we also recommend it for any large program. In this way, you can train staff to take over projects, in case a staff member gets a promotion or transfer, and so that the original staff can avoid burnout.

Next, you will have to decide upon a target audience. "Teens in such-and-such city" is a broad demographic. What groups will you be targeting with your advertising? Deciding upon a few target groups will aid in planning the remainder of your event. If, for example, you plan to contact all local high school guidance counselors and enlist their aid in promoting your program, you will want to find out what career training the students may already receive and look at a calendar of major school-related events. You want to expose teens to new ideas about vocations, but you also do not want to compete with a major sporting event. Take time to make these considerations about any group that you intend to target, including the library's patrons. Your colleagues at other library branches will be more open to helping promote your trade school fair if it does not interfere with any special event that they may be planning.

TIME LINE FOR PLANNING

Once you have established the date of your trade school fair and which staff members will work on the event planning, it is time to back-date your calendar. Three months prior to your event date, you will want to have your first team meeting. At this meeting you will create a planning document and brainstorm a list of potential vendors to invite. We have included our planning document from 2017 in appendix D. You will see that we found it helpful to brainstorm by both the type of program offered and by organization. We began with the area schools that we were familiar with and added in a list of vocations that our teen patrons had expressed interest in. For example, Jimmeka and Marie had previously worked with the cosmetology school Aveda Institute for another program, and already had a contact with the school. Aveda Institute was added to the list. We also knew that many of our patrons were highly interested in video games and might enjoy learning more about how they were created, so we did research to discover which vocational schools in our area offered such a program. (There will be more information about organizations to contact later in this chapter.) As well, you will want to use this meeting to create a schedule of future meetings and task due dates. As you do, you can go ahead and assign tasks to team members. In 2015 Marie was in charge of contacting our library system's marketing and communication staff to alert them to this event and to get advertising support. As a team, we had determined that we would need a response nine weeks before the event. Marie was responsible for reaching out to the marketing and communication staff early enough that they would have time to respond before our self-imposed due date. Jimmeka, who is an excellent graphic artist, took on the task of creating eye-catching flyers for the event and coordinating media exposure. Amy has strong research and communication skills, so she began the process of reaching out to local schools and training programs to discover what programs they offered. We encourage you to do the same: as you plan your event, assign tasks that play into your, and your colleagues', strengths. A full vocational program fair will be a big enough task to plan without having to learn new skills.

Next, designated team members will design flyers for advertising the event, while others collaborate with the library's marketing and communication staff. This collaboration allows for a unified and targeted marketing strategy. Any team members who are not involved in either of these tasks can use this time to continue cultivating a list of institutions to invite to the program. In this case, Marie communicated with the library's marketing and communications staff and received an outline of the support and contributions that they would be able to provide. Knowing the marketing and communication department's deadlines for disseminating information to various local publications in turn gave our team a deadline for flyer creation. We have included a sample flyer in appendix B. To keep the momentum going, we formally met again only two weeks later.

At the second meeting, ten weeks prior to your event, you will want to finalize the list of organizations and schools to invite to the fair and draft the invitation e-mail. You may find that your area is awash in vocational schools. If so, you are fortunate, but you will need to refine the list if you are using a community room or other space with limited capacity. You may find yourself at the other end of the spectrum because there are very few vocational schools in your area. In this case you might use time during the second meeting to brainstorm related organizations that you could invite. At another local library, the teen librarian held an event similar to our trade school fair, but included representatives of the armed services. You also should not neglect to contact your library system's job resource center librarians. They would be a great asset to invite to your fair and could likely tell you about local skilled trades training programs if you need further ideas. We suggest working together to draft a boilerplate invitation e-mail to send to schools so that you can present a unified front, and eliminate the possibility of forgotten details. We have included a sample e-mail in appendix C.

You will want to have the e-mail ready to send immediately following the second meeting. According to the time line used at ImaginOn, we sent the invitation e-mails eight to ten weeks prior to the Fast Track: Trade School Fair. Because we had a small team of staff working on our event, we divided the list and each of us sent eight to ten e-mails. Although we drafted a form e-mail for the initial invitation, we each responded to those schools that answered our invitations.

You will spend the next month conversing with trade schools and continuing to work on marketing. Two months prior to your event is when most local publications, such as parents' magazines or local-event papers, require submissions for their print calendars. Many online publications only need four to six weeks' notice to add an event to their calendars. Libraries are increasingly using software to plan and manage their social media posts; you would be well advised to use this month to set up some tweets, posts, and blogs to go live in the two weeks prior to the fair. By that time, you will be busy with all the immediate needs of the event and presenters. Why not take advantage of the tools at your fingertips?

The next date that you will need to include on your planning calendar will be one month prior to your fair. At this time, you will want to meet formally with your colleagues once again to draft e-mails to those schools who did not respond to the initial e-mail. Do not give up on a school simply because it did not respond to your first e-mail. We found that some schools were easier to contact via phone, whereas others responded to the second e-mail. Do not be shy; remember that you are asking these organizations and schools to come to your event to share information with the teens you serve.

Once you have all the schools confirmed for attendance, the next planning task on your time line will be to send yet another round of e-mails to teen organizations two weeks prior to the event. Now is the time to find volunteers to assist on the day of the event. Teens make excellent volunteers, but you might also reach out to your library colleagues. Even if they are unable to commit to the entire planning process, they may be willing to assist you on the day of the event. You will also want to invite teen groups to attend the fair. There are a number of groups that focus on connecting teens with positive mentors and future readiness, such as the CLAY (Career Leadership Academy for Youth) program administered by Goodwill Industries and the Boys and Girls Clubs. These groups are always looking for career and educational development opportunities for their teens. To help spread the word we have reached out to public high school guidance counselors, nearby alternative high schools, churches with established youth groups, YMCAs and YWCAs, and recreation centers. At ImaginOn, we kept a record of organizations that had scheduled visits within the past year and contacted each group's leader. We also left flyers in nearby public spaces such as bulletin boards at coffee shops, hospitals, and recreation centers. (Remember that all this was on top of the print/online marketing that our library's marketing and communication department assisted us in arranging.) If you haven't already done so, two weeks prior to your trade school fair is an optimal time to begin mentioning it on social media. Go ahead and begin posting or schedule your social media manager to drop posts at strategic times. Teens are drawn to visuals, so consider posting an image of the event flyer to Twitter, Instagram, or Tumblr.

One week later (seven days before the trade school fair), you should e-mail all your confirmed representatives. This e-mail will contain all the details for the day of the event, including explicitly spelling out what they can expect to receive from the library in support. If you have asked the schools to bring representative objects for their vocation, you will want to provide information about loading dock access. If you are an urban location, you will want to provide information about nearby parking garages or lots and pricing, and the availability of waivers (if you are able to offer them). We certainly offered as much support as possible to the schools to make it easy for them to attend, such as offering tablecloths or pens for their tables, and free parking for the representatives. Lay out the time frame in which you expect presenters to arrive and set up, and what time the event will be open to the public. During this last week leading up to the fair you will want to increase your social media posts and do any radio or television interviews.

Before you know it, you will arrive at the day before your trade school fair. We always prefer to be slightly over-prepared for programs and events, so we spend the day prior printing flyers or handouts for the event, creating and checking off items on materials-needed lists, and ensuring that all necessary tables and chairs are accounted for and in the room. We gather all the ephemera that is needed for the fair: pens, Sharpies, cardstock for name tents, Post-It notes, masking tape, charging cords for tablets and laptops, bottles of water and hard candies for the representatives, raffle prizes, raffle tickets, giveaways, and a few extension cords. We load these up on book carts that will be ready to roll in the morning. Because we knew that we would want to use this event to advertise other upcoming programs, we printed copies of our department's program calendar and extra copies of any flyers for special events.

All this preparation the day before the trade school fair leaves us feeling more relaxed on the day of the event. As at most libraries, day-before setup was not possible because other departments or programs were using the space. On the day of the event we arrived early to set up the tables and chairs in a horseshoe formation. We used cardstock to create name tents for all the tables. This allowed us to evenly space out the tables of the various trade schools. We placed video game development and massage therapy programs in between the two cosmetology schools so they would not end up next to (and competing with) each other. We left bottles of water and a few hard candies at each table for the presenters. They will be talking to teens and parents all afternoon and their throats will get dry. At our first two Fast Track: Trade School Fairs we offered popcorn to attendees; if you plan to do so this will need to be set up in advance, especially if you are popping your own. (If you're conflicted about whether to pass out popcorn, we can reassure you that we did not notice any decrease in attendance after we stopped offering it to attendees.)

By the time that you have everything set up, it will be time to begin welcoming the representatives from the schools and organizations. Volunteers come in handy to help with greeting the presenters and locating needed materials for them, or to man the loading dock entrance to let presenters in and out. On the day of the event, everyone's responsibilities will run together. There will most likely not be a break in between greeting the schools' representatives and greeting library patrons arriving for the event. We discovered that it was best if at least one of the main planning-committee members was not assigned to a table or the door, so that there was at least one knowledgeable staff person who could act as a floater and attend to any needs that arose.

Do not forget about your raffle, either: make sure that the greeter at the door is handing out tickets to those who enter, and remember to call for prizes every so often throughout the event. As a bonus, raffles are a great way to keep count of attendance at programs such as this one, as every person who enters gets one half of a ticket. All you will need to do after the event is count ticket stubs, and you will know how many people attended.

In the first iteration of the Fast Track: Trade School Fair, we hired a DJ to play music during the event and invited speakers to give a panel discussion. Although the DJ created a lively atmosphere and the panel of speakers contributed useful and engaging information, we ultimately decided that the effort was greater than the return. Even at a low volume, the DJ's music distracted from conversations about potential careers, and not many attendees wanted to pause their conversations with school representatives to listen to a panel discussion. You will learn what works best with your teen patrons.

MARKETING YOUR TRADE SCHOOL FAIR

After you have lined up all the institutions to be represented at your trade school fair, it is time to market your event to the community. As mentioned earlier in the chapter, you will want to decide on target audiences to help you best craft your message. For the original Fast Track: Trade School Fair, we knew that we wanted to target young people in our community ages sixteen to twenty-four. Having a part of our target age range include young people who would still be living at home, we wanted a flyer design and message that would be appealing to teens and to their parents. We did not include professional marketing pieces in our budget for the program, so we were relying upon a team member, Jimmeka, and our own hard work to promote it.

The Fast Track: Trade School Fair flyer has been completely re-envisioned each year, but we have included a sample of our flyer from 2015 in appendix B as an example. At that time, Microsoft Office Publisher and Microsoft Office PowerPoint were the best tools that we had at our disposal for flyer creation. By the time of the writing of this book, we had discovered Canva.com and were honing our skills in that medium. Although the visual standards for marketing to teens seems to change and evolve annually, a few things remain constant: teens are highly visual, so high-contrast graphics are a must. Teens have also become accustomed to reading short amounts of text or skimming longer pieces of text. Place your most important information in bold letters and consider the use of bullet points for any type of list. Finally, teens are often brand-loyal. Do not be afraid to use the logos of invited schools on your flyer, as that may draw more teens to your event. A good rule of thumb in flyer creation is to include all pertinent information in one place. Do not make your reader search for further information using a website address or QR codes. Make clear the time, date, and location of your program, and what they can expect to learn from attending.

Once you have designed your flyer, it is time to distribute it. Have all the libraries in your system display it in their teen areas and put it out via social media channels. Most libraries, as mentioned previously, have software or subscriptions to browser-based services that allow them to set up and plan posts to social media. Utilize this software to have posts go live at times when teens or their parents are likely to be checking social media: right after school, and late in the evening. Do not forget that social media users are much more likely to click on, re-post, share, or "like" an image as opposed to a text-based post.[3] There is no need to create more work for yourself; simply share the flyer image. In our experience, getting a teen patron or volunteer to share or re-post your image can add credibility to it, and lead to even more sharing and "liking."

Beyond sharing your flyer on social media channels, share your flyer in physical community spaces, such as the bulletin boards in coffee shops, or at other community youth-serving organizations such as recreation centers. E-mail copies of the flyer to guidance counselors at public and private high schools or drop off a stack of preprinted flyers at the schools for distribution and display.

Established print and broadcast media can also help you promote your trade school fair. Our inaugural year, one of our staff team members had a personal relationship with an employee at a radio station and arranged to go on the air to mention the event. Our library's marketing and communication team was willing and able to help us get the event description out to multiple local papers and magazines. Many local papers, especially free publications, will allow the library to list their programs and events in their "Calendar of Events" section for free. Blogs that feature events to participate in around town will usually allow organizations to post their event on the "Calendar" page for free. Take advantage of the free advertising; it is worth your time to submit.

Begin your advertising as early as possible. As noted in the time line for planning, the graphic design should be one of the first things that you accomplish. This way, you will have time to share flyers and information about the program early, at other related library programs. When you hold a "Meet a Professional" (discussed in chapter 3) program prior to the trade school fair, be sure to hand out flyers for your upcoming trade school fair.

When marketing for an event that you are putting a larger than usual amount of effort into, remain indefatigable. Send out flyers to any place that you think might display it and connect with all your contacts in your community. Reach out to youth group leaders who have visited your library in the past and personally invite their groups to the event.

EDUCATIONAL INSTITUTIONS TO INVITE

As mentioned above, you will need to develop a list of potential educational institutions to invite fairly early in the planning process. For inspiration, we share our complete list of Charlotte, North Carolina-based institutions in appendix D. Although you may not have the exact same institutions in your area, you should be able to find organizations in your area that offer similar programs. For example, you will not find a Charlotte Star Room outside of Charlotte; it is a singularly owned entity. You can, however, search for key terms such as "talent development classes" and [city name]" to find the same services in your own area.

We found that all the institutions we considered fell into one of three categories: community/technical college, vocational certification program, or skills training. When we began brainstorming, we were easily able to name the local technical colleges and add them to our list. We had course catalogs in the library that we could look to for information regarding which majors were offered. Although it is easy enough to look at your local community college's website and find a list of majors offered, it is more difficult to discover who would be your best contact. You could, of course, contact an institution's recruitment office, but it is likely that the student ambassadors or recruitment officers that it would send to your fair would be "big picture" people who would try to sell the college as a whole. The purpose of a trade school fair is to present technical, hands-on options for teens looking for a fast track into a career and who may not be interested in pre-baccalaureate associate's degrees that are designed to award credits to transfer into a four-year university.

Participants will want to hear details about individual programs. Contact heads of departments like public safety, early childhood education, dental assistantship, and game development. You may be able to make connections with the dean of an entire campus or of a division. Such a contact may be able to send multiple student and staff representatives to speak with prospective students in detail about the individual programs. When you look at a course catalog or website for a community college, the number of vocational programs offered may seem overwhelming. Try reaching out to other organizations first, then use the community college to fill in any gaps. For example, we learned that there is an automotive repair program offered through Universal Technical Institute in Charlotte, that also has ties with NASCAR. This is highly appealing to teens. We did not feel the need to duplicate this resource by also inviting representatives of community college automotive repair programs. (Although if you have a large space to fill with trade school offerings, you may lean toward quantity and options.)

Look at national technical schools that have campuses in your area. For these more narrowly focused schools, contact their recruitment offices when inviting them to an event. We learned that schools are often charged a fee to have a table at recruitment fairs, and that representatives were often excited to learn that the library is hosting a trade school fair that does not charge exhibitors. We found that we could offer them free marketing by placing their schools' logos on all our flyers and advertisements. These two incentives alone are usually enough to get a conversation started. (In the first year we did struggle somewhat with our inability to prove a track record of attendance for the program, but in later years we were able to confidently report large numbers of attendees, which further enticed schools to send recruiters.)

Beyond the larger technical colleges in your area, consider the smaller training or certification schools near your library. Look for institutions that offer specialized programs that can come and speak to your teens. One way to start this process is to search yellowpages.com (or similar search engine) for a given vocation. For example, you might search "massage therapy" in order to discover a local training facility, or "dental hygienist" for a training program. You may find that not every desired vocation is represented in a training facility near you. Do not give up or get discouraged; simply keep looking, and do not be shy about asking others for advice. If you want a dental hygiene program represented at your fair, ask local dentists' offices for recommendations. Their dental hygienists will be able to tell you where they received their training. We found our barber school representative upon the advice of a professional barber who came to the library for a "Meet a Professional" workshop. You might also find specialized training programs via billboards or bulletin boards around the city. We first heard of UTI (Universal Technical Institute) while watching a sporting event on television; it advertised that it offered NASCAR-level automotive care training at its institute. The very next week we e-mailed the school to ask for a representative at the Fast Track: Trade School Fair.

Do your teens love to draw their own comics or manga? Consider seeking out a graphic design program. Do your teens love to read about animals? Consider seeking out a veterinary technician program. We became very excited about technological trades and sought out a local coding group that offers certificates in a multitude of programming languages.

Do not neglect to include any careers specific to your area. A more rural library would be remiss to exclude a representative from 4H or other farming groups. A library in Los Angeles or New York City should go ahead and include representatives from talent development agencies. (Be highly selective when considering talent development agencies, because they often have a very high upfront fee structure with no guarantee of future employment.)

Any schools or facilities that offer structured classes leading to a degree or certificate are welcome additions to your trade school fair. Do not limit yourself solely to institutions traditionally identified as "trade schools." Look also to specialized schools that teach massage therapy, cosmetology, barbering, or computer technology. Between technical colleges, specialized schools, and other resources, you will have plenty of presenters for teens to hear from.

OTHER RESOURCES TO FEATURE AT YOUR FAIR

The first year that we planned a Fast Track: Trade School Fair, we were pleasantly surprised to find out that the College Foundation of North Carolina provided scholarships, grant money, and loans to students pursuing vocational degrees or certificates. Granted, we had never spent much time considering how teens could pay for an associate's degree or vocational certificate. Since beginning work in an urban youth-serving library, we have become much more empathetic to the needs and concerns of teens who may not be able to afford even the modest fees necessary to pursue these degrees and certifications. Some of the teens we have helped enter community colleges and certificate programs have been teens who were going to age out of the foster care system at age eighteen and would have no family financial assistance at all. Other teens graduating high school already had families to support. Upon graduation, they would transition from full-time-student moms to full-time-working moms and needed all the financial assistance they could get to care for their children. For these teens, it could be a deciding factor in their post-high school plans to know that they would have financial assistance if they chose to pursue a vocational certification.

We have included a booth for the College Foundation of North Carolina at each year's Fast Track: Trade School Fair event. You will find similar resources in your area. Investigate whether your state's College Foundation offers financial aid for trade school certification programs, and if any local agencies provide grants or scholarships for the vocational training programs as well. Often individual schools or programs will offer assistance.

As mentioned at the beginning of the chapter, a large part of the idea behind the Fast Track: Trade School Fair came when Marie discovered that Mike Rowe of *Dirty Jobs* fame had established a foundation to help teens pay for vocational training. We investigated it further, because we planned to request brochures or business cards for distribution at the library, and went so far as to put in a media request to see if Mike Rowe would like to come to our inaugural Fast Track. (He did not.) We discovered that the foundation does not print informational materials for distribution. When we visited his website (www.profoundlydisconnected.com) we were, however, able to gather information that we could share with our teens.

You might also choose to invite United States government agencies such as Job Corps. Another library in our area hosted a trade school fair in which they invited branches of the armed services to send representatives. Although we did not choose to invite them to our program, they are a natural fit for this type of event. Often, a young person receives valuable training while serving that can transition into a civilian career. The Job Corps is an especially helpful program, because it provides participants with certification in a vocation at the end of the program. As a bonus, participants are paid and receive room and board while they are in the program.

In our experience, we have seen teens who would be considered "at risk" enter the Job Corps and completely turn their lives around. Although they may have been directionless and possibly some were in and out of trouble in high school, Job Corps provided them with structure and training, and removed them physically from their environments.

Remember that this is a library-sponsored event. You will also certainly want to include a library table or booth displaying a variety of vocational-themed books, alongside any flyers you may have for upcoming vocational-directed programs. Consider offering students the opportunity to take online vocational aptitude quizzes. At our events, attendees were excited to learn the results. One teen told us that: "I found out that I might be good at massage therapy. I'd never have guessed that, and I'm going to look into it."

At the inaugural Fast Track: Trade School Fair, we had three library resource tables spread throughout the event space: a table with mobile devices for taking the assessment, a book display table, and a table for resources from our system's Job Help Center. In later years, we consolidated the books and the Job Help Center resources onto a single table. The Job Help Center resources let attendees to see what types of jobs are currently open in Charlotte, North Carolina, and to know that the library is there to assist them with finding a job once they have received certification. Having a few library-centered tables helps to remind patrons that the library is behind this wonderful program, and to highlight the resources you have to offer patrons concerning their career pursuits.

FOLLOWING UP

At the end of the program, consider having paper or electronic surveys available for participant feedback. Every library where we have worked has encouraged the collection of "stories of impact" on the community. These statements describe how a library service or program positively affected the participant. They make excellent blurbs for future event advertising. You can include these in your report to superiors to document the effectiveness of the program.

In addition, you will need to collect the names of the representatives who came to your program to share information, for writing thank-you notes later that day or the next. These notes of gratitude will leave the schools and programs with a positive impression of the library and will make them more eager to return next year (should you decide to make this an annual event).

Most important of all: at the end of the program, after you've sent out the thank-you notes, do not forget to reflect on your efforts and your team's hard work. Run a debriefing session and decide what worked well and what aspects of the program will have to be redesigned or eliminated in the future.

Recognize and thank any staff or public volunteers who assisted with your trade school fair. Then give yourself a good round of applause for all your hard work, and all the information that you brought to one location for your teen patrons.

CONCLUSION

Planning a trade school fair at your library may feel like a daunting task, but when you create a time line to schedule tasks, we hope that you will feel that it is doable. As we have established in previous chapters, this sort of program is vitally important to our teenage patrons. By sharing our journey from the very first planning and brainstorming session to the writing of the last thank-you note, we hope this chapter will help you on the way to planning a successful trade school fair for your library.

Notes

1. Brittney Johnson, "Labor Shortage Delaying Projects, Increasing Costs in Charlotte," March 20, 2017, www.wsoctv.com/news/local/labor-shortage-delaying-projects-increasing-costs-in-charlotte/504398245.
2. "Lifetime Earnings by Education Level." *Trends in Higher Education.* College Board, 2017, https://trends.collegeboard.org/education-pays/figures-tables/lifetime-earnings-education-level.
3. Catriona Pollard, "Why Visual Content Is a Social Media Secret Weapon, *Huffington Post,* May 5, 2015, https://www.huffingtonpost.com/catriona-pollard/why-visual-content-is-a-s_b_7261876.html.

7

"Teaching to a Career" in the Library

THE TRUSTEES OF WHAT IS BELIEVED TO BE THE FIRST public library in America, the Boston Public Library, wrote in their very first report to the City of Boston in 1852,

if the young machinist, engineer, architect, chemist, engraver, painter, instrument-maker, musician (or student of any branch of science or literature) wishes to consult a valuable and especially a rare and costly work, he must buy it, often import it at an expense he can ill afford, or he must be indebted for its use to the liberality of private corporations or individuals. The trustees submit, that all the reasons for which exist for furnishing the means of elementary education, at the public expense, apply in an equal degree to a reasonable provision to aid and encourage the acquisition of the knowledge required to complete a preparation for active life or to perform its duties.[1]

With this statement, the trustees formally stated what many in public library service already knew: the public library is the people's university. It is a place where any and all can come and have access to the continuing education materials that they may need after leaving the public educational system. Historically, the access to books alone was enough to satisfy most patrons' post-formal education needs, but today's patrons require more. They have come to expect more formal educational opportunities: classes and programs that teach new skills. No longer can teen librarians expect to spend their days staffing a stationary reference desk in the Teen section. Now they know that they will be with the teens, hanging out, messing around, and geeking out.[2] In the process, you will connect with teens and act as an informal mentor or instructor, doling out advice on homework, educational plans, and potential careers. Furthermore, you may find yourself orchestrating opportunities for these teens to receive actual training from a visiting presenter or educator within library spaces. In this chapter we will discuss some formats for formal learning that you might encounter, explain the benefits to both the teen patrons and the library, and show you examples of how public libraries across the nation successfully implemented programs.

TYPES OF LEARNING OPPORTUNITIES WITHIN LIBRARIES— MOOCS, LEARNING CIRCLES, PARTNERSHIPS WITH OTHER ORGANIZATIONS, AND LYNDA.COM

Although you are probably familiar with information literacy classes and programs, and may have taught some of them yourself, there are other types of learning opportunities that you might offer or facilitate in your library for your teens, such as MOOCs, learning circles, partnerships with other organizations, or online courses. We will discuss the benefits to both your teenaged patrons and your library in greater detail later in the chapter, but keep in mind all the previously mentioned reasons for introducing your patrons to vocational-readiness courses. There is a demonstrated growth in demand for skilled labor jobs in America, and our teen patrons must be poised to enter these fields upon graduation from high school. Even students who expect to eventually enter a traditional four-year university can benefit from the ability to secure gainful employment to help with tuition costs. As well as hosting a trade school fair in your space, your library could facilitate actual learning or certification opportunities for teens. Both methods are effective for introducing teens to a variety of skills and vocations that they may not be aware of as options.

The first type of course that we would like to discuss is the MOOC, or Massive Open Online Course. A long history of mail-based correspondence classes led to online distance-learning courses which in turn formed the basis of the MOOC. In 2011, Stanford introduced what many believe to be the very first MOOC: a form of online distance learning, with the freedom of a correspondence course.[3] Learners who had no affiliation with Stanford could register for these courses and complete them via electronic correspondence, generally at their own pace. Prior to this, online learning was still regimented: a set number of students affiliated with a certain university would watch either a live feed of a professor lecturing or recorded videos of lectures and then complete assignments that a professor would individually grade. In some cases, students would still be expected to arrive on campus at the end of the semester for an in-person final exam. With the advent of the MOOC, many of these steps became automated. Quizzes and tests were taken electronically and automatically scored by a computer. This allowed for many thousands of students to complete a course simultaneously. These courses have only continued to grow in popularity, and platforms have been developed specifically to support them, such as Coursera and edX. In 2016 alone, fifty-eight million people registered for at least one of over 6,500 MOOCs being offered.[4]

A MOOC typically lasts four to eight weeks and offers a certificate upon completion. Not only can a student explore undergraduate- or certificate-level stand-alone courses, but edX is now offering graduate-level courses as well, in its "micromasters" program. These are structured similarly to traditional master's degree programs that require the learner to complete a series of four- to eight-week long courses to earn the credential.[5] Can the public library support and encourage these learners? Are your teen patrons interested in this style of learning? Both questions can be answered in the affirmative. Although teens will likely have little interest in "Time Management for Personal and Professional Productivity," they may be highly interested in "Introduction to the Music Business," "Public Speaking," or "Intro to HTML/ CSS." We can support their attendance of these programs by offering study rooms or other quiet spots to work in. We can perhaps simplify the process for accessing our library's WiFi or internet computers. Does your library have a policy that blocks access to internet computers when outstanding fines reach a set amount? Consider advocating for your teen patrons and asking the administration for leniency to override that barrier, so that young people can use the computers for academic pursuits. We can also provide space and facilitation for small groups who wish to pursue a MOOC program in collaboration, by following the growing trend toward learning circles in public libraries.[6]

A learning circle is a group of people who gather at a set time and location to participate in a MOOC together. There are many benefits to this setup: having peers who rely on you (and on whom you can rely) can increase your motivation to continue in the course of study. These peers can provide feedback or assist with brainstorming solutions when questions arise. The library can additionally provide a facilitator (maybe you?) to help troubleshoot technology and help participants locate answers to questions. You do not need to be an expert in the field yourself; the professors leading the class will handle the content. You only need to be available to set up the room, provide technology support, and guide participants to resources that the library already offers. Although it was marketed to adults, the Charlotte Mecklenburg Library's University City branch saw teens registering for a public speaking learning circle that they offered. Teens were interested in the course because they would be giving presentations as part of their graduation projects or interviewing for jobs or schools. Offering a summer learning circle that would interest teens, such as "Intro to HTML/CSS," can provide you with four weeks of programs that prevent the summer slide.

An alternative to having library staff facilitate programs based on MOOCs would be to invite other community organizations or instructors to come to your library and instruct your teen patrons. Many of the desired skills, such as coding instruction, can be taught through partnerships with other community organizations that offer the leadership but are seeking a physical location to conduct programs. While at ImaginOn, we worked with a local high school robotics group, Queen City Robotics.[7] The group had mentors and instructors, eager participants, and supplies for creating robots. It lacked a meeting place where it could gather a dozen teens and a mini-fridge-sized robot. We created a partnership that allowed them to use ImaginOn's meeting spaces for planning, development, and building; in exchange, the group provided instructors for a weekly Java programming class for the public.[8] This relationship has continued for nearly three years. Now the lead adults also assist with our annual summer Maker Camp programs.

Along similar lines, the Girls Who Code movement is often full of willing leaders and eager participants looking for a computer lab or meeting room in which to gather.[9] The library can provide that space. By making an agreement with the group coordinators to allow your library patrons to participate in the programs in exchange for waiving meeting room rental fees, you are providing your teen patrons an opportunity to learn a valuable skill. Yet another group that could be invited to your location is Girls Build.[10] This organization teaches construction skills to girls. No matter where your library is located you could reach out to this Portland, Oregon-based group to ask for recommendations of similar organizations in your state. Refer to chapter 4 for ideas for professionals whom you can invite to speak to your teen library patrons about their careers and the training necessary to qualify for the vocation. Although the speakers will not be providing the full instruction, they will inspire your teen patrons to begin pursuing the necessary courses of study. Other educational community organizations are excellent resources for vocational instruction in your library. The group leaders or instructors are skilled in the instruction of various courses of study and can provide high-quality teaching to your teens. In addition, they often draw a guaranteed audience if they are associated with a well-known group. In exchange for something as simple as a meeting room for their own established group, you can guarantee access to programs for your own library teens.

If you are unable to commit to a multi-week MOOC or learning circle, or to create a relationship with a partner organization, you can still provide instructional opportunities for your teen patrons through online educational programs that can be completed on a single date. This may be as simple as providing your patrons with computers and internet access or organizing a program wherein you view an online resource together and then practice a skill or discuss as a group. A few recommendations for online, open access learning sites:

- *GCF Learn Free* (www.gcflearnfree.org) states that "if you're willing to learn, we're ready to teach."[11] The focus of this website is technology, and it provides courses at many different levels. A student can learn everything from Microsoft Word basics to graphic design to Linux programming language. Founded by Goodwill Industries, this resource's sole aim is improving employment-readiness skills for users. The colorful, vibrant site will appeal to teens—it does not have the feel of an overly serious job-seeking tool. Full of videos, tutorials, and practice exercises, this site can assist you with learning many Windows-based programs.
- *Khan Academy*'s homepage (www.khanacademy.org) proclaims that "you can learn anything. For free. For everyone. Forever."[12] "What started as one man tutoring his cousin has grown into a more than

150-person organization."[13] Khan Academy has hundreds of tutorial videos on dozens of different subjects. Although it originated as a site to teach higher-level math, it now includes science, history, art, and computer programming. As a bonus, you can register for a free teacher account and cultivate a custom playlist of videos to share with your patrons.

• *TED* (www.ted.org) stands for Technology, Entertainment, and Design. It began in 1984 as a face-to-face conference series.[14] Today, anyone, anywhere, at any time can access TED Talk videos via the internet. These short talks are meant to engage viewers and encourage outside-of-the-box thinking about technological developments, entertainment, design, history, and culture. As of the writing of this book, the newest video posted is "The Surprisingly Charming Science of Your Gut" by Giulia Enders. It will be replaced by an even newer video within days. Viewing TED Talk videos can get your teens thinking and talking about global issues, and encourage them to consider where they might fit. They will be motivated to see other young people (many TED Fellows are in their twenties and thirties, and very relatable) accomplishing great things. This is also an excellent resource for instructional videos in design techniques, for teens who may be contemplating a career in design.

• *Hour of Code* (www.hourofcode.com) was created by Code.org and is "a nonprofit dedicated to expanding access to computer science and increasing participation by women and underrepresented minorities."[15] This website provides detailed curriculums and fun, free practice exercises that teach code to students online. Its Hour of Code program is a complete course in coding that can be experienced in approximately one hour. In our experience, it takes most teens and young adults less than one hour to run through. The courses advance through alternating video interviews of celebrities and teen programmers and puzzles solved using Scratch programming. This provides an engaging experience for users. It does not hurt that the puzzles are all themed around popular apps such as Plants vs. Zombies.

• *Learning Express Library* must be accessed via a library subscription. It grants users access to dozens of occupational career exams, such as Physician Assistant Certification, Air Traffic Controller Certification, the Firefighter Practical Exam, the Law Enforcement General Exam, and the Plumber's License Exam. Users of the database can take the exams an unlimited number of times for practice and receive feedback and advice for improving their scores. In addition, teens and young adults can peruse its extensive database of informational articles on hundreds of different careers.

- *Lynda.com* (www.lynda.com) is a subscription website whose mission is "to help you learn the skills you need to achieve your full potential." Furthermore, it is "a leading online learning platform that helps anyone learn business, software, technology, and creative skills to achieve personal and professional goals."[16] Now owned by LinkedIn, this website helps thousands of users learn new skills. Most of its video tutorials cover computer software and hardware, but there are also courses on such topics as becoming a photographer or small business owner, as well as many other professions. If your library subscribes to Lynda .com, your patrons can access it for free.
- *Universal Class* must be accessed via a library subscription. It offers dozens of video courses on everything from Positive Parenting to Veterinary Assistance. Each course awards a certificate of completion at the end, which could assist young adults in their search for employment. These courses are excellent for introducing teens and young adults to a variety of vocations without the investment in a technical college's tuition.
- *State-based workers' resources sites* are available online. Many states have excellent state-based workers' resources sites. For an example, see the KansasWorks site at www.kansasworks.com. Potential workers can research careers, find training, and connect with potential employers on the sites. You can find a full list of these types of sites in appendix E.

BENEFITS TO TEEN/YOUNG ADULT PATRONS

As you can see, there are numerous benefits to teens available at their local public libraries. The greatest challenge may be letting teens and their parents know about these opportunities. Once the word is out, people will be sure to flock to the programs. Our mission is twofold: we must somehow get the information to teens and their parents that vocational jobs are on the rise, and then also inform them of all the programs and training available for no cost at their local library.

Although it seems abundantly clear that there are benefits when teens choose to participate in the programs and trainings that you offer, there is an even greater good: when teens try their hand at a new career idea, participate in a learning circle, complete an online training course, or take part in an internship facilitated by the library, they are participating in a *risk-free failure opportunity*. This may not be a commonplace phrase. It refers to the invaluable opportunities that public libraries provide to teens to fail without lasting consequences. For example, when a teen attempts to write a program for a Makey Makey in a library program, they can simply enjoy the experience. They have not paid for the Makey Makey or spent hard-earned money on lessons in programming—and are able to engage in the afternoon's coding activity without worry. When teens log into Lynda.com with their library card numbers, they can take an unlimited number of courses in a wide range of subjects without investing a cent. If they discover that the subject does not interest them as much as they expected, or they fail and must retake the course, there is no personal loss other than time. In these ways and many more, we provide teens with risk-free failure opportunities. Think of Thomas Edison, the innovator behind the modern incandescent lightbulb, who is famously quoted as having said, "I have not failed. I've just found 10,000 ways that do not work." We teen librarians can provide those 10,000 failure opportunities that lead them to the 10,001st experiment that succeeds spectacularly.

BENEFITS TO THE LIBRARY

Overwhelmingly, library system mission statements speak to empowering communities and providing learning opportunities—look to these library mission statements from the Charlotte Mecklenburg Library, Beaverton City Library, Louisville Free Public Library, and Multnomah County Library:

> Improve lives and build a stronger community.[17]

> Foster community and enrich the lives of individuals through learning, engagement and connection.[18]

> Provide the people of Louisville and Jefferson County with the broadest possible access to knowledge, ideas and information, and to support them in their pursuit of learning.[19]

> Empowering our community to learn and create.[20]

By giving our teen patrons a chance to further their education at the library, we are fulfilling our library's mission to our community. Public libraries rely on public funds to remain open, and we can only do that if taxpayers continue to vote to fund us. When we can bring stories about how the library is positively impacting young people's lives, we build equity in their hearts and minds. City and county councilmen will remember that the library helped a certain number of young adults in our community successfully prepare to enter the workforce, and may be more inclined to grant the library any needed increase in funding.

Library staff members also benefit from MOOCS, learning circles, and other online courses on a more individual level. One of our favorite aspects of these types of programs is that they are usually prepared by, and perhaps led by, a professional who works outside of the library. For us, it is much less work to simply advertise an event and then set up a room than it would be to plan a presentation and activity to lead. We are raving fans of presenters. In addition, the material that is prepared by a professional in the field is likely to be much more accurate than our best research could provide, and partnerships are built when a library works with another organization to provide a service to its patrons.

A little later in this chapter you will read about the learning circles offered at the Charlotte Mecklenburg Library. As an example, one of Marie's colleagues directly e-mailed a professor at Michigan Institute of Technology regarding an online course. The professor was amenable and worked with the librarian to offer the course to library patrons free of charge. In addition, their conversation became more of a collaboration, and he offered resources and tips about the best ways in which to facilitate the course.

You will also read about the Louisville Free Public Library, and the partnership that it developed with Code Louisville. Like any good partnership, both parties were able to give a service, and both parties received a benefit. The library provided access to Treehouse, a coding language learning library, and Code Louisville provided instructors to facilitate classes. Library patrons could take the classes for free, and Code Louisville received access to library computer labs in which to offer the programs.

Last and certainly not least, the community that the library serves receives the benefit of an increase in the portion of the population ready to enter the workforce and fill vocational jobs. In the Louisville example that we will present, the program emerged because of the lack of workers in the area available and trained to fill certain positions. The library was able to partner with Code Louisville to provide the necessary training, and Louisvillians were able to find employment. In Charlotte, an economic task force was convened after a report was published by Harvard University. Charlotte was found to have the lowest opportunity for upward mobility in the entire United States. The report identified a lack of college and career readiness among residents as one of the top reasons for this ranking.[21] The Charlotte Mecklenburg Library has been conscientiously planning library programs to help fill that gap.

CASE STUDY:
CODE LOUISVILLE AT THE LOUISVILLE FREE PUBLIC LIBRARY

Code Louisville at the Louisville Free Public Library was launched in the fall of 2013. This twelve-week program was so successful that it was awarded a federal grant of $2.9 million in the fall of 2014, with the goal of expanding the program to other library systems nationwide. This initiative was started in order to fill a gap in the community: every ninety days, there are nearly one hundred unfilled junior software development jobs in the Louisville area, and Louisville's population was not trained to fill these positions.[22] The partnership between the Louisville Free Public Library and Code Louisville (along with monetary support from a few other local and state government agencies) sought to solve that problem by offering free courses on coding and software development to the public. At its inception, the main keys to the partnership were that the Louisville Free Public Library provided the license to Treehouse, an online code-teaching software platform. In fact, all cardholders can access Treehouse with their library cards, regardless of whether they are currently in a Code Louisville session. KentuckianaWorks, a statewide employment assistance agency, referred people to the library for the training and Code Louisville provided the instructors to guide students through the courses.[23]

The program itself is twelve weeks long, and students must commit to all twelve sessions. Currently, the program has outgrown library resources and is now run entirely by the Code Louisville nonprofit. Although you can still find a brief description of the program on the library's website that hearkens back to its creation as a library partnership program, the link directs you to the Code Louisville website for program registration.[24] An excellent indicator of success is seen when the program has a waitlist that is too long for the library to handle by itself.[25] Working together, Code Louisville and Treehouse's Code-to-Work program provide training for participants at a library location. The Code-to-Work program will "take someone with no computer programming experience, teach them how to code and help them land a job in the tech industry—all without a degree."[26]

Matt Ferguson is a success story from one of the earliest iterations of the Code Louisville program. Formerly employed as a paralegal, he completed a twelve-week program in front-end web development in 2014. Soon after the course ended, he was able to work with a recruiter to find a job in the field. Note that although jobs are not guaranteed as a result of completing the program, Code Louisville does offer connections between the program and potential employers. As a result, many individuals who complete the program do land jobs in their desired fields.[27]

Although this program was targeted at adults, it is a topic that would be of interest to many teens. A similar program at your library could draw many teen participants. Matt Lorenzo of the Cupertino Library in California, for example, developed a one-night computer programming event for teens that reached maximum registration very soon after registration opened.

CASE STUDY:
PEER 2 PEER UNIVERSITY LEARNING CIRCLES
AT THE CHICAGO PUBLIC LIBRARY

Peer 2 Peer University (P2PU) is a nonprofit organization that helps to bring libraries, online courses, and learners together. It trains librarians and other community activists to facilitate learning circles in their neighborhoods. What is a learning circle? It is a group of individual learners who gather together in a shared physical space to participate in an online open educational resource.[28] MOOCs, discussed earlier in the chapter, are good examples of an online open educational resource. Online open educational resources are typically brief (six to eight week) courses that offer a certificate of completion or a digital badge at their conclusion. Traditionally, students would participate in an online open educational resource on an individual basis.

For many of you reading this book, taking an online course is not intimidating. You own at least one computer or tablet and have wireless internet in your home. You will also, however, be familiar with the other side of the digital divide. Many of your patrons may not have a computer available in their homes, or it might be shared among many family members. They may or may not have internet access at home. For them, taking a course online might be daunting. P2PU trains librarians (and other community members) to facilitate online courses for groups of students by connecting potential learners with the space and technology that they need for success. Most of the time, this takes place in a library community room and requires library-owned Chromebooks or laptops for use during the program.

The Chicago Public Library was among the first libraries in the country to adopt the learning circles program model, in 2015. A doctoral candidate, Christiane Damasceno, spent two months with both facilitators and learners to gain a deeper understanding of the program and how it works. She wrote that an outstanding characteristic of the learners was their self-motivation. When asked why she pursued an online course in public speaking, one participant stated that she felt it had the potential to make a positive impact in her life.[29]

So far, a majority of learning circle participants across the country have been adults, but many courses could have teen appeal. In Charlotte, the head of a library branch is going to market its upcoming Public Speaking Learning Circle to both teens and adults. At the end of the senior year of high school, Charlotte teens must give a presentation that is a requirement for graduation. Many teens will gain confidence and necessary skills by participating in the learning circle. Not to mention that public speaking skills will be invaluable when a teen or young adult is applying for and interviewing for employment.

CONCLUSION

Although we chose to write in detail about only two libraries, the Louisville Free Public Library and the Chicago Public Library, they are only two of many libraries offering learning opportunities. We have heard about a learning experience related to solar power development that is offered in Allegheny County, Pennsylvania. Using grant funding, the library was able to offer seven teens a $100 per session stipend for a program that included both classroom instruction and hands-on experience. At the end of the experience, which the library dubbed a "fellowship," the teens had gained important real-world experience in the development of solar power initiatives in the community. Because the teens had to apply and interview for positions in the program, they also gained general workforce-development skills that could transfer into future employment opportunities. We heard from a library in Pueblo, Colorado, that offers "internships" to teens sent to the library by the local Workforce Center. Their Workforce Center works in partnership with the library: it sends youths to the library to provide them with volunteer service opportunities, and the Workforce Center pays them. The teen librarian who answered our survey told us that the teens who participate not only get to assist with program planning in the library, but they also gain experience with applications for the program, interviewing, and working under supervision. We heard from a teen librarian who held what sounds to be a very fun event, in which teens were invited to work as groups in a timed competition to see who could take apart and then rebuild a car engine in the shortest amount of time. He facilitated the event and invited local schools that offer automotive repair certification courses, a local race team, and a local car club.

Throughout history, public libraries have been considered "the people's university," a place where learners can come together and explore new ideas or training. Although the methods have evolved into offering online learning opportunities in addition to in-person training, the intent behind the effort has not changed at all.

Notes

1. Boston Public Library, *Report of the Trustees of the Public Library to the City of Boston*, 1852. Reproduced in Jesse H. Shera, *Foundations of the Public Library: The Origins of the Public Library Movement in New England, 1629–1855*. Chicago: University of Chicago Press, 1949; repr., Hamden, CT: Shoestring Press, 1965, 267–290.
2. Nancy Friedman, "Word of the Week: 'Homago,'" *Fritinancy* (blog), March 10, 2014, http://nancyfriedman.typepad.com/away_with_words/2014/03/word-of-the-week-homago.html.
3. Andrew Ng and Jennifer Widom, "Origin of the Modern MOOC (xMOOC)," 2014, www.robotics.stanford.edu/~ang/papers/mooc14-OriginsOfModernMOOC.pdf.
4. Dhawal Shah, "By the Numbers: MOOCS in 2016," *Class Central*, December 25, 2016, https://www.class-central.com/report/mooc-stats-2016/.
5. Jill Fisher, "Top 4 FAQ about the Micromasters Credential," *edX* (blog), February 7, 2017, https://blog.edx.org/top-4-faq-micromasters-credential.
6. P2PU, "P2PU Presents: Learning Circles," https://learningcircles.p2pu.org/en/.
7. Queen City Robotics, "Our Sponsors," http://queencityrobotics.org/who-we-are/sponsors.
8. The group ended up hosting their annual statewide robotics tournament at Imagin-On, and opened attendance to the general public at no charge. This introduced robotics and coding to many families who might not have otherwise known about them. Sometimes partnerships are gifts that keep on giving.

9. Girls Who Code, https://girlswhocode.com.
10. Girls Build, www.girlsbuildpdx.org.
11. GCF Learn Free, "About Us: Who We Are," https://www.gcflearnfree.org/info/aboutus/who-we-are.
12. Khan Academy, https://www.khanacademy.org.
13. Khan Academy, "About," https://www.khanacademy.org/about.
14. TED, "About," https://www.ted.com/about/our-organization.
15. Code.org, "About Us," https://code.org/about.
16. Lynda.com, "About Us," https://www.lynda.com/aboutus.
17. Charlotte Mecklenburg Library, "About," www.cmlibrary.org/about.
18. Beaverton City Library, "About Us: Administration: Mission and Strategic Plan," https://www.beavertonlibrary.org/323/Mission-Strategic-Plan.
19. Louisville Free Public Library, "Our Mission Statement," www.lfpl.org/mission.htm.
20. Multnomah County Library, "About Us: Multnomah County Library Priorities 2016–2018," https://multcolib.org/about/priorities.
21. Alana Semuels, "Why It's So Hard to Get Ahead in the South," *The Atlantic*, April 14, 2017, https://www.theatlantic.com/business/archive/2017/04/south-mobility-charlotte/521763.
22. Code Louisville, https://www.codelouisville.org/.
23. Kate Silver, "Get Cracking on Code," *American Libraries*, March 30, 2015, https://americanlibrariesmagazine.org/2015/03/30/get-cracking-on-code.
24. Louisville Free Public Library, "Computer Classes," www.lfpl.org/computer-classes.htm.
25. Urban Library Council, "Code Louisville/Treehouse," https://www.urbanlibraries.org/code-louisville-treehouse-innovation-1069.php?page_id = 423.
26. "Code Louisville to Expand Training for Technology Jobs With $2.9 Million Federal Grant," October 30, 2014, https://louisvilleky.gov/news/code-louisville-expand-training-technology-jobs-29-million-federal-grant.
27. Silver, "Get Cracking on Code."
28. "About P2PU."
29. Christiane Damasceno, "When Seekers and Rebels Meet (Or, My Experience Studying the Learning Circles)," *P2PU* (blog), June 14, 2017, http://info.p2pu.org/2017/06/14/when-seekers-and-rebels-meet-or-my-experience-studying-the-learning-circles.

8

Partnering with Schools and Other Organizations for Vocational Success

WE HAVE SPENT MUCH OF THIS BOOK THUS far detailing ways in which you as a teen-serving staff member can help your patrons prepare for a career from within your library. In this chapter we will talk about expanding your service focus outside the library walls. By working with local guidance counselors, teachers, and other community partners you can further assist teens with their career goals. The library provides resources to help teens achieve these goals, but often teens are not aware that the library is ready to provide this support. Through a strong partnership, school and public libraries can team up with each other and with other community organizations to provide teens with a support network.

In this chapter we will take you through the process of partnering with outside organizations and schools, starting with how to reach out and form the partnership. We know that libraries are considered "third spaces" to school and home—a place where teens gather after school and on the weekends for recreation and leisure. We will discuss a few ways that you can easily identify and reach out to other "third spaces" in your community. Further, we will advise you about how to develop those partnerships in a way that is healthy and beneficial to all parties. We will then take an in-depth look at a partnership between the Charlotte Mecklenburg Library and CLAY Leadership Academy at Goodwill centers and a partnership between a school media center in Loudon County, Virginia, and students enrolled in the school's Occupational Course of Study.

We will also explore ways in which you can get the whole family invested in a teen's vocational-readiness development. The support of parents helps to ensure that a teen participates in a career-readiness workshop series. The marketing looks a little different when reaching out to parents, but the same events should appeal to both parties. With minimal effort, you can double your marketing reach in the community when you appeal to both teens and their parents.

Once you have established the partnerships with other organizations and parents of teens, you will be well-positioned to provide superior assistance to teens working to achieve extra credit or graduation projects. You can continue to provide excellent research assistance, but add assistance in resume development and interview skills. We will look in-depth at the assistance that the Charlotte Mecklenburg Library is providing to teens working on major graduation projects. Partnerships like this make life easier and better for teens in that county.

Although teen librarians across the country are already doing great things for teens and their vocational readiness, we can multiply our effectiveness when we partner with outside organizations and schools to support our youth patrons through mutually beneficial relationships, outreach, parental communication, and our support of extra credit and graduation projects.

REACHING OUT TO FORM A PARTNERSHIP

The first step in creating a partnership with an outside organization is to identify the organizations or schools with which you would like to create a relationship. Nearby schools are certainly easy to get in touch with, but who else is in your community is serving teens? Are there after-school programs for at-risk teens near you? Nationwide, there are YMCAs and Boys and Girls Clubs that offer after-school programs for teens. Ask your colleagues and teen patrons where else young adults gather after school. Beyond the organizations that offer only after-school activities, there are also youth-serving resident programs, such as group homes, youth counseling centers, and juvenile detention centers.

We have been fortunate to find a great many fellow youth-serving organizations and programs organically. We both formerly worked in the Loft in ImaginOn, which is the teen-focused department within an entirely youth-focused public library. We would facilitate group visits from schools and other groups year-round. In the course of working with the groups who came to us, we would make contacts and acquaintances with group leaders. We cultivated a list of names and e-mail addresses of groups that frequently visited us and would e-mail them personal invitations to events that they would believe to be beneficial for the youth with whom they worked. For example, there was one group leader who told us that she was particularly interested in having programs at the library to introduce her teens to technology. She knew that many of the teens she worked with had limited or no access to digital tools in their homes. Every time we knew that the Loft was offering a program in coding, internet safety, or resume-drafting, we would e-mail to give her a heads up, and she would often find a way to bring her group to the programs. The CLAY Leadership Academy (which we will discuss in greater detail later in the chapter) is a group whose students were specifically interested in college, technical school, and vocational-readiness programs. We made sure that its group leaders knew about any programs we offered that were intended to prepare teens for life post-high school. These two groups were just a few of the partnerships formed by Loft staff.

In addition to organically created partnerships, we actively sought out and developed partnerships in our community. We heard from teens about other locations they frequented after school. We also noticed items in local publications that featured fellow youth-serving organizations. Occasionally the library would be invited to attend or participate in another organization's event and learn about them that way. In *Serving At-Risk Teens,* authors Angela Craig and Chantell L. McDowell dedicate a chapter to forming partnerships. They write that "to become an integral part of a youth facility, libraries are advised to learn the facility's routine, keep abreast of any changes in its operation, and to accommodate those changes if possible. Flexibility will go far when working with a community partner that serves youth."[1] We can't understate how important this is. You cannot go into a meeting with a potential partner with a fixed agenda. You must go in with an open mind and first listen to the group leaders and learn about the organization's goals for its teens. Once you understand what their program currently offers and what types of library programs it may be interested in, you can then begin to invite the group to events at your library.

Finally, youth services roundtables in your community bear mentioning. There might not be one in every community (they are more likely to be convened in larger urban areas), but if one exists, a teen librarian should be involved. Like a Rotary Club or Lions Club, these roundtables usually meet once per month or per quarter to provide a forum for sharing ideas and creating collaborations. Every person sitting at your table at each meeting is a potential partner for programs inside or outside of your library's walls. In addition, the other people attending the roundtable may work for organizations that are also deeply concerned about the well-being of youth in your community. These are terrific people to brainstorm with or discuss ideas about any upcoming programs or initiatives your library is considering offering.

Between groups that approach you and groups that you seek out, and by putting yourself out in the community through participation in roundtables, you will find a wealth of potential partner organizations that care about "your" teens just as much as you do. Working together benefits both your library (via increased program attendance and community visibility) and the other organization (who find a new field-trip destination and can take advantage of free programs for their teens led by library staff).

OUTREACH

So, what about the teen-serving organizations that cannot come to the library? Those organizations are best served through library outreach. When approaching an outside organization to establish an outreach partnership, the same rule applies as when approaching an organization to create an in-house partnership: flexibility, flexibility, flexibility. Say, for example, that you always schedule your programs for 4:00 pm. That is how it is always done, has always been done, and will always be done (we are exaggerating slightly for effect). Then you discover the youth detention center up the road always has an outside activity at the same time. It has scheduled its indoor activities for late morning. Do you turn down the opportunity to serve these teens because they are unavailable in the afternoon? We hope your answer would be that you would find time in your schedule to visit the center in the late morning a few times a month. Here's another example: you know that your Arduino programming class is very popular with the patrons at your library, and that programming is an up-and-coming skill. However, the youth counseling center down the block does not allow its residents to have access to computers at this stage in their rehabilitation. Do you turn down the opportunity to serve these teens because what you consider to be your best program will not work at that facility? Of course not. You can work with the center to develop an alternative program that fits its needs and restrictions, and that still teaches similar skills, such as paper circuits or paper programming. There are all sorts of screen-free coding activities that allow youth to learn computational thinking skills without touching a screen or keyboard.

Fortunately, vocational-readiness programs are usually adaptable and can be taken outside of library walls fairly easily. Often, all you need is a library staff member to present the information or a single visiting presenter. For example, a staff member can certainly provide information on building a resume or interview skills. If the facility restricts computer use for its participants, resumes can be drafted by hand on paper. Make sure to ask the facility beforehand whether you are allowed to bring your own paper and pencils or if you must use materials provided by them. Be sure to get approval for any resume-writing books that you may wish to bring along. Interview skills and public-speaking programs do not require any materials at all. A further vocational-readiness program that you may consider would focus on business and social etiquette and attire. There are social skills that an incarcerated teen or group-home resident may not have been exposed to. The teens in your outreach program might benefit from an outside figure such as a teen librarian helping them to navigate proper interview and work attire for when they look for their first jobs. Not every outreach program will be in a facility where the youth are restricted. We have also been on outreach visits to apartment complexes where the teens are restricted only by lack of means of transportation. When parents or other caregivers are unable to give their teens rides to the library, and the city bus does not come near enough to their residences, teen library staff must go to the teens. With these programs you will have much more flexibility. Because it will not be necessary to run extensive background checks on each adult, you could bring along a professional from the community for a "Meet a Professional" program. Because the teens will be allowed to use computers, you can bring a set of training laptops and assist participants with resume creation or guide them through a vocational aptitude quiz.

No matter the size of your community, there are likely to be at least a few after-school programs near your library. The goal of these programs generally is to keep children safe, and to provide enrichment activities while their parents are busy with work or other activities during the after-school hours. Some programs are run through the students' schools and some are run by other private or not-for-profit organizations such as the Boys and Girls Club. In all these cases, the individuals in charge of these programs may be searching for new ideas to keep the students engaged and enriched. Therefore, after-school programs are a perfect opportunity to present programs to a group of students who are excited to learn about new topics and try out the new gadgets and technology that librarians can bring along.

Through outreach, you can have a positive impact on many more teens than you could within your four walls. You can reach teens who are currently detained for various reasons and help them learn and grow and discover post-detainment goals. Outreach may feel slightly one-sided: you are physically coming to the group and providing library programs, often with library materials. However, you cannot measure the amount of goodwill and community improvement that will come from this time spent out in your community.

EXTRA CREDIT AND OTHER PROJECTS

When we began research for this book in spring 2016, we sent a survey to a YALSA distribution list and heard back from teen librarians across the country. A majority of respondents replied that they offered basic job-readiness programs such as resume assistance and interview skills. One respondent replied that she offered "Job Help" as an advertised program and that teens in her area could register online for an hour one-on-one with the teen librarian to work on resumes or to conduct practice interviews. Another respondent told us that she holds "open office hours" when she is available in the teen space in the library. All her teens know that she is willing and able to provide drop-in job help. We are confident that these librarians are only providing snapshots of the invaluable services that teen-serving library staff provide to their patrons across the country daily.

One memorable young woman, Jeneva, was a regular patron of the Loft at ImaginOn. By the time that she graduated high school, every single staff member felt personally invested in her academic life. She would come to the Loft three or four afternoons every week to work on homework until her parents finished their workday. Each of those afternoons she would set up her laptop and notebooks at a table situated just behind the staff reference desk. From there, we would talk about procrastination and try to help her develop time management skills, help her access Tutor.com for assistance with tough math problems, proofread her essays, sign her up for practice

SATs and ACTs, and when it came time, talk through her post-high school options with her. This informal mentorship relationship allowed us to come alongside a teen as they worked on homework and other projects, and infuse real-world advice into our interactions. You can do the same at your library and truly make a difference in young peoples' lives. With your support, they can earn higher grades and reap more extra credit points. In addition, you can provide advice that could drastically impact their post-high school lives by steering them toward local educational opportunities or vocational options if these are the best fit for them. In the case of Jeneva, we helped her to thoroughly think through her post-graduation options and to discover that for her eventual course of study—a bachelor's degree followed by a master's degree program in library science at the University of North Carolina at Greensboro—she could save some money by earning an associate's degree at the local technical college first.

On the other hand, a library can partner with schools to provide extra credit opportunities. In 2013, we planned a program for Banned Books Week that would involve a viewing of the film *The Hunger Games* followed by an interactive discussion mediated by a local professor of children's literature. A month prior to the program, we reached out to local high school English teachers and media specialists to both let them know about the event and to tell them that we would be dispersing tickets to students who needed to show proof of attendance for extra credit. On the day of the event about a dozen students asked for proof of attendance for their English classes. In this instance, the program came first and we reached out to local schools second. You could easily flip that scenario, though, and begin by forming a relationship with the school. Once you have determined what it desires and needs, you can more pointedly target it when offering programs with potential for extra credit.

Students often ask for opportunities to earn community service hours at the library. This is another opportunity for the library to assist students as they strive to fulfill their school requirements. We often only have volunteer opportunities for teens and adults who can commit to a certain number of months of volunteering because the volunteer program requires staff time for training. Yet, students often only need a few service hours per semester or maybe a total of ten to twenty over the summer months. Therefore, once-a-quarter or once-a-month service project programs can be a great opportunity for teens to earn a few service hours in a safe environment where they already feel comfortable. These one-off programs may be quick projects that benefit your library (such as crossing off barcodes on weeded books or organizing books for an upcoming book sale) or projects that benefit another organization but which take place at your library (such as stuffing envelopes for the local school fundraiser or making holiday cards to give to the elderly served by the Meals on Wheels program in your area).

When thinking about how vocational-readiness programs might fit into the realm of extra credit, consider reaching out to your school district's Exceptional Child programs. In Charlotte, North Carolina, there is an "Occupational Course of Study" for exceptional children who are capable of graduating with a standard diploma but require a smaller student-teacher ratio and more focused programs than those of more typical curricula. At the conclusion of the program, youth receive a standard North Carolina diploma and graduate prepared for the technical workforce. Some of these students go on to earn full vocational certificates. Teachers of these classes are often able to secure a school bus to come to your library and participate in vocational-readiness programs, and the instructors are often glad to partner with libraries to provide this training. In addition, the instructors may be open to granting extra credit to students who attend your evening or weekend programs.

CASE STUDY: GRADUATION PROJECTS AT CHARLOTTE MECKLENBURG SCHOOLS

In Mecklenburg County, North Carolina, all high school students must complete a substantial graduation project to receive their diplomas. It consists of four parts: a research paper demonstrating research skills and writing skills; a service learning experience project that demonstrates the use of knowledge and skills in a meaningful way to accomplish a goal; an oral presentation on their project presented to a review panel; and a portfolio to document tasks, record reflective thinking and insights, and demonstrate responsibility for learning during the entire process.[2] We want to draw your attention to the two parts of the graduation project that the public library can play a part in: the research paper and the service learning project. One of the beauties of the graduation project is that teens who invest themselves in it truly do learn skills that are applicable to their lives post-graduation. The extensive research paper sharpens the research skills needed for technical college or traditional university work. In addition, the service learning project provides an opportunity for students to hone and practice their workforce skills. Marie recently received an e-mail from a local high school student who wished to complete his service learning experience by volunteering or interning at ImaginOn. This is not uncommon. The Charlotte Mecklenburg Library is seen as a positive force in our community, we have an established teen volunteer program, and we provide a safe, indoor, air-conditioned environment. The teen wrote an impressively professional e-mail, and we in turn provided him with a valuable workforce experience.

There are three ways the public library can support teens as they do the work necessary to complete a service learning experience: we can provide teens with professional communication advice and training, assist with practice interviews, and can go so far as to provide the internships themselves. From both the formal survey that we sent out while doing research for this book and our many dozens of informal conversations with teen-serving library staff across the country, it seems many of us are already providing many opportunities for teens to learn how to build resumes and how to interview. In Charlotte, North Carolina, teen librarians specifically work on resume building and public speaking with teens when assisting them with their graduation projects. However, your library may choose to go above and beyond, and provide the internship opportunity itself for your patrons.

The opportunity to interview for and complete an internship in the library provides multiple benefits to both participants and the organization. This process allows them to gain real-world experience applying for jobs, and the internship itself provides an opportunity for risk-free failure. Ideally, teens will enjoy the internship and thrive. However, if they feel they're not suited for library work, they can end the relationship without any damage to their fledgling resumes. In Charlotte, the entire graduation project must fit together. This means that students who wish to intern at their local library branches as part of their graduation projects will also complete a research paper related to the career of librarianship or to a current issue involving libraries. These are yet more ways the internship is mutually beneficial to the library and the teen. Students can complete their service learning experiences in a safe, friendly environment and learn about a career that they may not have known much about previously. In return, the library gets a volunteer to assist with daily tasks and programs and, as a bonus, the library staff get to show a young person how multifaceted and rewarding a librarian's job is. Over the course of the internship the library will, ideally, gain a raving fan who will advocate for the library in their communities. Between the programs that we are already providing in resume writing and interview skills, and the internships that we could begin offering, public libraries are ideally poised to help teens with career building through such specialized programs as graduation projects.

CASE STUDY: CLAY LEADERSHIP PROGRAM PARTNERSHIP WITH THE CHARLOTTE MECKLENBURG LIBRARY

The Charlotte Mecklenburg Library Teen Services staff partner with the CLAY Leadership Program at the Charlotte Goodwill Industries headquarters. The Career Leadership Academy for Youth (CLAY) is a program designed to nurture and build successful leaders among its participants. Teens apply for the program and once accepted receive academic support and coaching, leadership development, life skills development, career preparation, career experiences, horizon broadening events, and vocational coaching.[3] The program runs the entire length of the school year, and the coordinators hold weekly meetings for the teens. At each meeting the participants receive a meal, affirmations, and recognition of successes from the week prior. The teens in attendance are attentive and motivated. They are fully invested in the program and have assurance from their leader-mentors that the evening's activities will positively affect their academic or vocational careers.

This partnership formed organically. While planning for the inaugural Fast Track: Trade School Fair, we researched other youth-serving organizations in our area in order to invite groups to attend. The year prior a representative from CLAY attended our library system's Teen Services retreat day to tell us about its program, so that we might refer teen patrons. From this presentation, we knew that the program was very career- and post-high school-focused. Once we had reconnected with the presenter, Kwain, we learned that he had the resources to take teens in his program on day trips, and we invited him to come to the Fast Track: Trade School Fair. On the day of the fair, he arrived with about a dozen teens. They were among the first participants to arrive and stayed for nearly the entire program. After the program, Kwain took the time to e-mail our staff and thank us for inviting his teens, and to let us know that it fit perfectly into CLAY's program. From there, we continued the conversation through e-mails and in-person meetings as to how the library could continue to support CLAY's goals.

One evening, we represented the public library as we assisted the teens with their vision boards. Every year, CLAY kicks off its season with a vision board program so that they can help the teens focus their energies and attention on their personal goals. Before the partnership with the library, the CLAY leadership utilized poster board and discarded magazines for this project. We came in and taught the teens and their leader-mentors how to use online resources to create digital vision boards. CLAY had access to entire classroom sets of laptops and knew that its teens needed to develop digital literacy skills. It was a natural partnership for us to come in and help them to use these resources with their teens. On another occasion, a library staff member helped to proctor and administer a practice SAT exam. As a benefit to the library, Kwain would occasionally lead career-readiness or motivational programs at the library (often especially geared toward young men). This partnership is mutually beneficial and sustaining. Not only do teens in the library and teens in CLAY have twice as many resources as they did before, but Goodwill Industries, the parent organization to CLAY, offers many resources to young adults who are searching for careers or vocations, and so the partnership can sustain library patrons past the age of eighteen.

CASE STUDY: TUSCARORA HIGH SCHOOL LIBRARY INTERNSHIP

When we began work on this book, we surveyed dozens of librarians across the nation who work with teens. We were delighted when Mary told us about her work with teens in her high school media center in Loudon County, Virginia. The library staff work closely with transition teachers and job coaches to customize vocational programs for students with special needs. They interview the students and evaluate them individually to determine not only their abilities but also their interests. The library staff and the special needs teachers try to accommodate every student who is interested, but Mary tells us that sometimes they have more students interested than they have work that needs doing!

Mary told us how rewarding she found customizing jobs to each student's abilities and interests and providing teens with intellectual or developmental disabilities with opportunities for success. She shared the story of one of her students:

> Jon was a student who worked with us several years ago. Jon has autism and is very withdrawn. He rarely interacted with students or staff, walking through the halls with his hood pulled down over his face and never

making eye contact with anyone. He came to work in the library, and we discovered his love of manga comics. He loved to draw them and was quite good at it. We put him to work making bookmarks, cutting the paper, drawing the comics on them, laminating them, and displaying them. His love of manga provided a context for him to begin interacting with other students and gave him a sense of accomplishment when his bookmarks were used and appreciated by others. He came out of his shell, took off his hood, and walked with more confidence throughout the halls.[4]

Mary is not alone in her enthusiasm for helping teens with disabilities to gain confidence through internships or volunteer opportunities in the library. We have seen this in action with one of our most dedicated teen volunteers at our library. This teen is quite shy and has a difficult time reading. Because of his disability, he was not confident shelving books (a typical volunteer task at our library), but we discovered that he loves comics and drawing. He became an enthusiastic creator of flyers and a focused participant in our science events. Teens like these make our work worthwhile. When we see them succeed in internships or volunteer work in the library, we can know that we have made a definite difference in their lives.

CONCLUSION

Working with teens in a library setting is a rewarding experience. Imagine, then, multiplying that reward by partnering with schools and other youth-serving organizations in your area. These partnerships may come easily and organically, or you may need to seek them out. No matter how these partnerships come to fruition, you will want to ensure that they are mutually beneficial. In the case of the Charlotte Mecklenburg Library's partnership with the Career Leadership Academy for Youth, the library went to CLAY's location to teach digital literacy skills and the leadership of the CLAY group came to the library to participate in programs and to lead career motivational classes. The partnership may be mutually beneficial: in the case of Tuscarora High School in Virginia, librarian Mary is using her library internship program to build confidence in the school's special needs students. To see the benefits of this program, we must look into the future, when the students have graduated with the skills and confidence necessary to gain employment in their communities. This also applies to the Charlotte Mecklenburg Library's partnership with Charlotte Mecklenburg Schools to support high school students pursuing their graduation projects. The benefits of this partnership are seen when the students succeed and graduate ready for post-high school work or study. To go beyond traditional partnership opportunities with schools or after-school programs, you could consider expanding into institutions such as youth incarceration facilities and treatment centers. Through these partnerships, you can easily double or even triple your impact on your community's youth and their post-high school opportunities.

Notes

1. Angela Craig and Chantell L. McDowell, *Serving At-Risk Teens: Proven Strategies and Programs for Bridging the Gap* (Chicago: American Library Association, 2013), 64.
2. Charlotte Mecklenburg Schools, *Graduation Project: Home,* www.cms.k12.nc.us/cmsdepartments/ci/grad-project/Pages/default.aspx.
3. Goodwill Industries of the Southern Piedmont, *Career Leadership Academy for Youth,* https://goodwillsp.org/train/youth-services.
4. Teen Vocational Programs at Libraries (April 26, 2017), survey distributed by ALA Editions.

9

Evaluation: The Importance of Creating and Using Measurable Outcomes

E HOPE THAT YOU ARE NOW EXCITED ABOUT your own series of vocational-readiness programs, and that you anticipate continuing the programs into the future. Maybe your library is ready to take that next step towards starting a teen volunteer or internship program. To ensure continuity and to make a case for future programs, you will need to track results. Tracking can use quantitative or qualitative methods. It is likely you will find a use for both types of research when reporting the results of your programs.

In 2010, a teen in Mecklenburg County, North Carolina, stood in front of the county commissioners and spoke eloquently of how her internship at the library helped prepare her for her collegiate studies and future career. She asked the council to consider continuing, if not increasing, funding to this vital community organization. At this time, the Charlotte Mecklenburg Library was facing significant budget cuts to library programs. Personal anecdotes attesting to the effect of library programs are just one type of data that you can gather. In addition, you can gather observations about impact, statistics from program attendees, and survey results.

Why should library staff take extra time to collect stories of impact and statistical data when their work days are so busy? This information has the potential to make a difference not only in your department or individual branch, but on the future of the entire library system. Teens who attend library programs and then become employed and empowered young adults demonstrate positive growth to the community. The next time that your department, library, or system needs to argue for funding, how will you go about illustrating the impact your work is having on the young people in your area? How can data be used as a tool to advocate for the importance of libraries?

Do not let money be your sole reason to take an evidence-based approach to programming. Beyond the excellent argument for demonstrating the benefit of funding, measuring the success of library programs has inarguable and innumerable benefits to library patrons, the library itself, and the library's partner organizations. Together, through strong career-readiness programs for teens, the library can work within and without to better the entire community.

MEASURING THE IMPACT

It can be difficult to accurately measure program outcomes. Results are sometimes interpreted subjectively and criteria vary from library to library and study to study. When Marie worked at a library in South Carolina years ago, outcomes were measured solely by number of attendees at a program. At her small, outlying branch, these low attendance numbers at teen programs meant that staff were not dedicated to teen services and the teen program had a paltry annual budget. What was not shown on paper when only attendance numbers were tracked, however, was the enthusiasm of the small but loyal group of teen patrons. At the outlying branch, the public library was one of a very limited number of educational venues for teens. The library was located a half-hour's drive from the nearest shopping mall, and nearly a forty-five-minute drive from the nearest community college. When the branch did offer a monthly teen program, they had five to six teens who would faithfully attend. There was simply no way to show the impact on the community's teen population in attendance numbers.

Working in Charlotte, North Carolina, we originally tracked both attendance numbers and stories of impact. A story of impact is an anecdote that illustrates a specific instance where the library helped a patron achieve a personal goal. For example, if a staff member assisted a patron with creating an e-mail account and hunting for a job online, and the patron returned to the library the following week to share that he or she had received an invitation to interview, the staff member could report that as a story of impact. The library maintains a database on its staff intranet called STARS (STories About Real Success), where staff can enter these stories of impact. These cannot be developed through fleeting interactions. Library staff members must invest time in their patrons to garner a story of impact. We have found that it can be difficult to collect stories of impact from teenaged patrons: members of this age group do not always return to tell us about their successes and you cannot always elicit a complete story of impact in the course of a single afternoon or program.

To assist libraries with sharing their collected stories of impact on their communities, the Public Library Association developed Project Outcome. Project Outcome is a free online tool that provides surveys and outcome graphs to public libraries to help them track the impact they have on their communities. The Charlotte Mecklenburg Library is one of many dozens of libraries nationwide now employing this tool to help assess the value of their library programs.

COLLECTING AND UTILIZING COMMUNITY FEEDBACK

Over the years, we have come across many different ways that libraries seek to measure the outcomes of various programs. Most commonly, libraries collect the number of people attending each program and report these statistics in a formal report at the end of each month or at the end of the year. Libraries often use these attendance statistics to draw conclusions about whether the community was interested in the topic of the program or whether the program had merit. However, most of us have had the experience of planning a program that seemed like it would be beneficial to the community and yet no patrons attended. We then write other stories in our heads about why no one showed up. These could be anything from "I should have marketed the program better," to "it must be because of the cold, rainy evening that no one wanted to make the trip to the library tonight." In this type of situation, we do not know why no one attended. However, before offering programs of this type in the future, or worse, deciding not to offer programs of this type in the future, it is important to gather some information from the community that the library serves. In such cases, outcome measurement must move beyond numerical statistics to be truly useful to library staff.

Collecting feedback from your community can be done in a variety of ways, most commonly through comment cards, informal discussions with staff, scheduled focus groups, and surveys. These methods could be used to evaluate any aspect of library operations. In this section, we are referring specifically to evaluating vocational programming for teens.

Comment cards can be a way to collect information from the community that does not require significant staff time and effort. Comment cards and boxes can be left out in a space where teens and their caregivers will be likely to see them. To be useful, comment cards should pose specific questions: For example, "what types of programs could the library offer for high school students to help them consider careers they might like to pursue?" A whiteboard or chalkboard can be set up in the teen area with a question for teens to answer. Data on this board can be regularly collected so space can be cleared for new responses. Keep in mind that soliciting feedback in a way that requires little staff involvement may result in a low response rate, and you might not receive enough feedback from your community to be useful for program planning. In addition, not all participants will be likely to answer a voluntary survey and this would result in responses that are not representative of an entire patron base.

Informal discussions with patrons are often a good way to keep your pulse on changing community needs. You might hear ideas that are less likely to emerge from other methods of collecting feedback. While working at the Loft at ImaginOn, we found our best program ideas were a result of discussions we had with teens after we sat down next to them and started up conversations. Teens learned to trust us and were more likely to open up about issues they were facing in their lives. Teachers and parents of teens often visit the library to seek advice from staff, which provide terrific opportunities to learn how the library could play a role in assisting these families. Staff can also ask patrons about potential career programming topics or gauge their interest in a potential volunteer or internship program.

Focus groups can gather a great deal of data from a cross-section of patrons using your library system. A focus group could be geared at collecting patron feedback about a broad range of topics relating to the library or focus on a specific topic such as career programming at the library. The library can invite a specific age group to a focus group, which allows discussion to focus on the needs of that particular patron group. A focus group facilitator can guide the discussion and lead the group back to the question if the discussion veers off track. Teens appreciate incentives for participating in these types of discussions: These could include candy, pizza, or other types of giveaways. If your local schools require a certain number of volunteer hours per semester or year, a focus group is a great way for students to earn a service hour or two while the library forms relationships with new teens and collects valuable feedback from a broad range of teen patrons.

A library's Teen Library Council or Teen Advisory Council serves as a type of focus group because it can regularly provide feedback to staff and help them develop programs. These teens may also be likely to attend the resulting programs. Although this group of teens is invaluable to a library, it should be noted that it represents only a small sample of the teens in your community (often those who are already more likely to become involved in community groups and events), so this feedback should be balanced with another way of collecting data from a larger cross-section of the community.

Creating and circulating a survey for teens can yield a great deal of useful data. A survey does not require a huge investment in staff time, can be sent out in a variety of ways, and provides anonymity for the participants. The survey can be brought to community partners who can assist the library in getting these surveys completed by a variety of teens who may not normally set foot through the library doors. Importantly, a survey must be written with great care to ensure the data collected will have practical applications for the staff soliciting this data. There are countless articles and books on how to write and construct surveys, but below we have included some general tips of the trade.

The ideal question accomplishes three goals:

- It elicits a response that pertains to the topic it is intended to explore.
- It doesn't touch on other concepts.
- It means the same thing to all respondents.

Harvard University's Program on Survey Research offers the following guidelines designed to help compose survey questions:

- Avoid technical terms and jargon. Words used in surveys should be easily understood by anyone taking the survey.
- Avoid vague or imprecise terms.
- Define things very specifically.
- Avoid complex sentences. Sentences with too many clauses or unusual constructions often confuse respondents.
- Provide reference frames: Make sure all respondents are answering questions about the same time and place.

- Make sure scales are ordinal: If you are using a rating scale, each point should be clearly higher or lower than the other for all people.
- Questions should measure one thing. Double-barreled questions try to measure two (or more) things.
- Answer choices should anticipate all possibilities. If a respondent could have more than one response to a question, it's best to allow for multiple choices.
- If you want a single answer, make sure your answer choices are unique and include all possible responses.
- Avoid questions using leading, emotional, or evocative language.[1]

Here are additional tips from the Association of College and Research Libraries for creating evaluations:

- The evaluation form should only ask for information that program organizers plan to use in some way.
- Participants are more likely to return forms that are brief and easy to fill out.
- It is helpful to ask someone not familiar with the event or program to test the questionnaire in advance.
- Program organizers should consider providing contact information for participants to follow up if they have questions or additional comments.[2]

To ensure that the information the community provides will remain anonymous and confidential (if anonymity isn't guaranteed, state so explicitly), staff must be careful about how feedback is solicited, collected, and utilized.

Michael Quinn Patton created a developmental evaluation to be used by those evaluating social change initiatives. The process is meant to deliver real-time feedback that can assist in continuous adjustments as needed. Developmental evaluation "supports innovation development to guide adaptation to emergent and dynamic realities in complex environments. Innovations can take the form of new projects, programs, products, organizational changes, policy reforms, and system interventions."[3]

Developmental evaluation is a useful tool for assessing teen programming. These programs grow because of the welcomed involvement from the participants. In fact, the most successful teen programs at our libraries are those that involve the patrons themselves in the development and facilitation process. Traditionally, program evaluation in libraries has been conducted by those outside of program facilitation, such as a branch manager or division supervisor. In contrast, developmental evaluation "positions evaluation as a job duty of the program deliverers," such as librarians or program assistants.[4] To clarify, the staff involved in developing and facilitating will evaluate the program with the assistance of the participants.

Once you have collected valuable feedback from your community in a way that best suits your programs and patrons, your library can begin to put it to use to plan for future programming. What types of programs are your audience interested in attending? How are interests and needs related to career programming, volunteer experiences, or internships? What goals do they have and what type of assistance do they need to achieve these goals? This information provides a foundation for building successful program series and one-time events. Compile the information collected in a way that makes it easy to sort results, grouping similar responses while separating dissimilar ones so no information will be missed. Using the resulting report, discuss the findings with the staff in your department, your manager, and even the library director, all of whom can assist you in analyzing the feedback in a way that will result in actionable steps. Patrons will be gratified when they see some of their suggestions become reality.

TELLING THE LIBRARY'S STORY

If your library is only "set up to collect evidence, measure data and generate reports, you may be ignoring a crucial step of the process which involves demonstrating how the outcomes relate to the inputs."[5] We must dig deeper to confirm that the library has had significant impact. Telling the library's story using anecdotes and personal accounts from community members can help connect the dots back to the library's work.

Beyond quantitative data sources are anecdotes about how the library has impacted individuals. Perhaps you have heard a story about a child struggling with reading who gradually improved and scored in the 95th percentile on his end of grade test after reading to a therapy dog weekly at the library and checking out a tote bag full of books each week. A teen who dropped out of school and was spending too much time at the transit station, connects with a teen librarian who helps him search for a job, learn interview skills, write a resume, and now is managing a hotel a few blocks from the library. These are the stories that help the library shine, and we should be collecting, recording, and sharing them any way that we can. These stories bring to life all the work library staff do each day in a way that statistics never could.

A simple formula for telling the library's story includes the following details:

Description. A short description of the patron at the center of the story (i.e., John, a recent high school graduate who has become a regular in the teen room this summer).

Issue or challenge. A short description of the issue or challenge they are facing. For example, a new school year was starting and John mentioned he was sad not to be returning to school with his peers. When we asked him about his plans, he said he was considering community college, but he thought he had already missed the deadline so he was going to have to wait until the following year.

Action. What did the library staff do to assist this patron with this issue? Julie, our teen services librarian, pulled up the college website for John and looked at the deadlines, only to find that the enrollment period had come to an end; however, Julie called up the admissions office and explained John's interest. She asked if there was anything John could do at this point. The admissions officer said John could come in and meet with her to talk about getting enrolled so he could still take a shorter half-semester class this fall. After the call, Julie and John talked for a while about his interest in taking classes and browsed through the course catalog together to talk about his interests.

Result. What was the result? John came back the following week to tell Julie about his trip to the admissions office. Julie helped John look at his options for financial assistance during that visit. Now in his second semester of school in the mechatronics program, John regularly visits the library to study for tests and work on his homework. He always checks in with the staff and his old friends in the teen area before finding a computer on which to do his work.

Telling the library's story can be done extremely well with words, especially with a skillfully written story demonstrating an impactful resolution. Pairing a story with a photo of the patron showing off his or her success can be even more powerful. A video recording of community members speaking in their own words can serve to truly illustrate what the library has done to enrich their lives. In 2016, the Charlotte Mecklenburg Library published a video featuring individuals answering the simple question, "What does the library mean to you?" One individual featured is a young girl who is shown reading a braille book. She explains that the library has allowed her to check out books in braille and to learn to read to her family. Now she is preparing to volunteer at an elementary school to teach other children to read. Viewers can infer that without access to high-quality braille books at the library, she may have never developed the love of reading that is inspiring her to give back today. This quick several-sentence story is told in her words, in her own voice.[6]

A story that illustrates the library's impact on community members shows how an individual is empowered and gains a new understanding about themselves or their abilities. Here are a few examples from our own experiences in libraries over the years:

- Jailah spoke about her desire to join the Air Force, asked for assistance with building her resume, and for help researching activities, such as volunteering, to prepare her for life after high school. She participated in the library's July and August Resume Building pop-up programs. Jailah eventually submitted her application for a position at Publix and did wonderfully with her interview. She also applied to be a teen volunteer.

- One of the program coordinators from the Goodwill CLAY program told us that after attending the Fast Track: Trade School Fair in March, several of his students followed up with representatives from the participating schools. He told us that one of his students plans to attend the Carolina School of Broadcasting and two other students have enrolled in the Aveda Institute. The coordinator told us that the fair had a significant impact on the students in the CLAY program. He said they were particularly intrigued by the 3-D printer the CPCC Engineering Department demonstrated and that the students continued to talk about it.

- A teen who was once a regular at the Loft stopped by and asked for help looking for a job. She also shared that she was pregnant and needed the job to support her child. Loft staff worked with her over the next few weeks, as well as with her mother, who stopped by with her a few times. The teen came in to share the good news that she was hired at the McDonalds in Huntersville. She was very excited, and we were happy she shared the great news with us!

- Mike was a regular for many years at the Independence Regional branch. He wasn't sure what he wanted to do after he graduated from high school. He eventually applied to the Job Corps and was accepted. We invited him to be a part of the panel discussion at the Fast Track: Trade School Fair. He was enthusiastic about sharing his experience in the program. One of the questions to the panel was, "Are you considering pursuing further education?" Mike answered that he was having trouble finding a job currently because he needed more experience to demonstrate his knowledge and, therefore, he was looking for some type of internship or apprenticeship that might allow him to gain experience. When we saw Mike later in the afternoon, he told me that after the panel discussion, the department chair of the HVAC Technology program at CPCC approached him and told him that they have a Workplace Learning program that places students in positions with employers for one semester so that they can gain the experience needed to further their careers. The department chair told Mike that employers often hire these students for permanent positions. He encouraged Mike and complimented him on his speaking skills and determination. Mike later let us know he was accepted into a Workplace Learning program that will help place him in a job in his new field.

Once you have numbers, statistics, and outcome stories, you will be able to present the information to your constituents, stakeholders, administration, and governing boards. Infographics are a fantastic way in which to present your accomplishments. Linda, a school librarian in Colorado, was faced with a challenge to take two decades worth of numerical outcomes for her school district and present them to constituents. The data reports were full of industry jargon, and technical terms. They were also unwieldy: two decades of data filled many spreadsheets. So Linda created a legal-sized infographic that summed everything up and presented it to her stakeholders. The results of using the infographic to share information were so successful that Linda was invited to give a presentation at the 2016 ALA Midwinter Conference in Boston, Massachusetts. At that conference, she gave four pieces of advice for creation of infographics:

- Put the numbers in context. She recommends saying "nine out of ten" rather than "90 percent," or presenting the numbers by referencing pop culture: "seven times as many libraries as Starbucks stores."

- Choose the appropriate way to visually display your data. Linda recommends that we slow down and think about whether a pie chart or a bar graph will more accurately and impactfully show our data.
- Simplify and establish a focal point. When you have many years of data to work with, it is tempting to try to fit all of it into your infographic. However, it may be more effective to showcase only the data related to one significant impact on your community.
- Don't make people work too hard to find information. Add labels to your images and graphs to help tell people what they are looking at.[7]

A well-executed infographic can help to tell your library's story to a diverse group of community members who may not initially be familiar with your library's services. It can be easily shared electronically, inserted seamlessly into presentations, or distributed to staff to use for talking points.

Fortunately, there are numerous free online tools to assist you in infographic creation. Some of our favorites include Canva.com, Venngage.com, and Piktochart.com. They are all browser-based, so there is no need to download any software. You simply create a free account, choose a template, and insert your own data. A librarian with moderate technological savvy can create a professional-looking infographic in the course of an afternoon.

Canva.com is hands-down our personal favorite. It allows you to save your creations in your own free account and to share them. There are literally dozens of templates to choose from. Beyond flyers and infographics, you can quickly and easily create graphics for your blog, website, and more. There are many graphics and fonts built into the site and you can add your own images as well. Unfortunately, there are a few drawbacks to Canva.com. First, not every template design is free. The user must pay attention to the template examples as they browse to ensure that they do not choose a costly template. Canva.com will not stop you from expending creative energy on a design; the cost is not applied until you are ready to download and/or share. At that moment you may discover that you must pay a fee. Another con is that it is awkward to add your own images to a design. Canva.com lacks a copy-and-paste function, so users must save desired images to their computers and then upload the images into Canva.com before they can add them to their designs. Overall, however, the ease of its plug-and-play templates for infographics overcomes Canva.com's slight disadvantages; we consider it the leader of browser-based infographic creation resources.

Venngage.com and Piktochart.com share similar pros and cons with Canva .com, although with what we consider slightly lowered usability and flexibility. Both are free to use and have a strong focus on infographics. A further advantage of both is that they will not allow you to begin work on a template if it is not free, therefore potentially saving you time and effort. A shortcoming of these two websites is that they offer more limited design choices and less customizability than Canva.com. Whereas Canva.com's options and freedom to customize may seem overwhelming, Venngage.com and Piktochart.com can feel limiting. Among the three websites, though, we are confident that you can find a design that works for the presentation of your information.

CONCLUSION

Over the years, we have found that evaluation is a crucial component of ensuring our program offerings are intentional and remain relevant to those we serve. Evaluating the purpose of what your library offers for teens will help determine if there is a way to improve any services or offer new programs. Data collection and evaluation may sometimes fall to the bottom of an ever-growing to-do list, but we urge you to discuss options for evaluating your programs with your supervisor or teammates and come up with a plan to collect this invaluable feedback. We promise that some of those stories of impact from your own library will stick with you for many years to come.

Notes

1. Harvard University Program on Survey Research, "Tip Sheet on Question Wording," https://psr.iq.harvard.edu/files/psr/files/PSRQuestionnaireTipSheet_0.pdf.
2. http://acrl.ala.org/IS/is-committees-2/resources-for-officers-and-committee-chairs/program-evaluation-forms.
3. "Thirty Days of Teen Programming," http://yalsa.ala.org/blog/2015/04/15/30-days-of-teen-programming-develop-your-evaluation-skills.
4. Ibid.
5. "Three Keys to Improving Your Program Effectiveness Success," *Social Solutions,* www.socialsolutions.com/blog/three-keys-to-improving-your-program-effectiveness-evaluation.
6. The Charlotte Mecklenburg Library Story, www.youtube.com/watch?v=ULIZT2LT7vA.
7. Sanhita SinhaRoy, "Data Visualization for the Rest of Us," *American Libraries Online,* January 9, 2016, https://americanlibrariesmagazine.org/blogs/the-scoop/data-visualization-for-the-rest-of-us.

10

Collection Development: Selection Tools and Criteria

COLLECTION DEVELOPMENT IS A VITAL COMPONENT of excellent library programs. Books, ebooks, and online resources provide an extension of the program that teens can take home with them. When developing your collection with vocation-readiness in mind, you must work to keep the selection fresh and vibrant. Teens may not naturally be drawn to nonfiction career-focused books unless they can see the relevance to their own situations. In addition, we recommend supplementing the traditional nonfiction career books with fiction in which teens or young adults are working in vocational fields.

BOOKS TO ASSIST TEEN-SERVING LIBRARY STAFF

Understanding adolescent brain development is a great foundation for developing quality programs and services tailored to your teen patron base. Over the years, we have learned a great deal about how teens think and how they make decisions. Although each teen is unique and should be treated as an individual, the stages of brain development are similar for all teens. Importantly, the rational part of the human brain does not complete development until the age of twenty-five. Most information processing takes place in the amygdala until this time, which means teens are experiencing each life challenge in a way that involves more emotion than that of the average adult. We believe that we can better advocate for the teens we serve if we can appreciate their unique perspective.

Some of the titles in this section are meant to help library staff develop an understanding of adolescent development, such as *Age of Opportunity: Lessons from the New Science of Adolescence*. Other titles address developing library services that will appeal to a teen audience. For example, *Cooking Up Library Programs Teens and 'Tweens Will Love: Recipes for Success* offers step-by-step instructions for designing and facilitating cooking programs for teens at your library. *Teen-Centered Library Service: Putting Youth Participation into Practice* presents a more holistic approach to building self-esteem and self-awareness while helping teens to form meaningful connections at the library. *Emerging Adulthood: The Winding Road from the Late Teens through the Twenties* specifically covers the period of life between adolescence and adulthood. The author, Arnett, notes that the years between eighteen and twenty-nine are filled with exploration of the self as young people experiment with a variety of career options. His insights into the way young adults in this age range think can help us to design library services that will not only appeal to them, but also have the most impact.

Sometimes the teens who could most benefit from library services are the most resistant to our efforts to connect them with resources. Trusting a librarian can be a difficult for teens who have felt let down by other adults such as parental figures or educators. We recommend checking out *Serving At-Risk Teens* by Angela Craig and Chantell McDowell, an ALA publication that includes an array of practical tips and programming ideas to incorporate into your offerings for teens.

Beyond the Skills Gap: Preparing College Students for Life and Work and *The Future of University Credentials: New Developments at the Intersection of Higher Education and Hiring* are specifically related to helping young people prepare for the challenges of today's job market. These titles will arm librarians with information about the current workforce that adolescents are about to enter. Keeping our eye on the job market in our area was helpful when working with teens at the Charlotte Mecklenburg Library. It was useful for us to know when local employers were hiring so we could steer teens towards those openings. For example, each spring Carowinds (a local amusement park located about fifteen miles south of downtown Charlotte) would post openings for seasonal positions. They employ a great number of teens each summer, supplying many young people with their first real job experiences. Because we knew the deadline to apply to these positions, we could mention this opportunity to teens who we knew were looking for employment.

The titles below may provide some new information as you work to serve the needs of teens in your community:

The Age of Opportunity: Lessons from the New Science of Adolescence, Laurence Steinberg (2015)

Beyond the Skills Gap: Preparing College Students for Life and Work, Matthew T. Hora, Ross J. Benbow, and Amanda K. Oleson (2016)

Cooking Up Library Programs Teens and 'Tweens Will Love: Recipes for Success, Megan Emery Schadlich (2015)

Emerging Adulthood: The Winding Road from the Late Teens through the Twenties, Jeffrey Jensen Arnett (2014)

The Future of University Credentials: New Developments at the Intersection of Higher Education and Hiring, Sean R. Gallagher (2016)

Serving At-Risk Teens, Angela Craig and Chantell McDowell (2013)

Teen-Centered Library Service: Putting Youth Participation into Practice, Diane P. Tuccillo (2009)

Teen Services 101: A Practical Guide for Busy Library Staff, Megan P. Fink (2015)

The Teenage Brain: A Neuroscientist's Survival Guide to Raising Adolescents and Young Adults, Frances E. Jensen and Amy Ellis Nutt (2016)

The Whole Library Handbook: Teen Services, by Heather Booth and Karen Jensen (2014)

BOOKS THAT ALLOW TEENS TO VISUALIZE THEMSELVES IN A VOCATION

It is vitally important for teens to be able to imagine themselves working at a vocation before they can feel confident about making it a goal. Sometimes, teens can see themselves in a career when they visit a parent or other adult at their workplaces. Other times, young people can participate in an internship that allows them to get a sense of what a certain career entails. However, there are also times when a teen does not feel connected to their parents' careers, or have the opportunity to participate in an internship. In these cases, books can help to fill the gap. We are reminded of the words in the opening to the *Reading Rainbow* television show: "I can be anything! Take a look; it's in a book."[1] By reading about potential vocations, teens can get an idea of what it might be like to work in that career.

Some of the most entertaining books about vocations feature a main character or subject with an interesting career. In *Maker Pro: Essays on Making a Living as a Maker,* teens read about more than a dozen up-and-coming professional makers. The makers share their pathway to success, discuss any challenges they had to overcome, and give plenty of encouragement to potential makers. This easily approachable book of bite-sized stories is a great resource for teens dreaming of starting their own businesses or inventing new products. *Sous Chef: 24 Hours on the Line* and *Relish* describe what it is like to work in the fast-paced restaurant business; the authors of these books all write from experience about what it is like to be young and working at the entry-level in their careers. *Relish* is unique among these books: it is a graphic novel! One final book in the genre of "through their eyes" experiences is *In Their Shoes: Extraordinary Women Describe Their Amazing Careers.* This book is another collection of essays that also has profiles, sidebars, lists, and helpful tips to inspire young adults just getting started on their career paths.

Once a teen becomes enthusiastic about a career that he or she has read about in one of the previously mentioned titles, teen-serving staff can offer a young person one of the following books to get them started on the pathway to a rewarding vocation. In *You Majored in What? Designing Your Path from College to Career, The Teens' Guide to College and Career Planning, The Art of Work: A Proven Path to Discovering What You Were Meant to Do,* and *Undecided: Navigating Life and Learning after High School,* the authors provide step-by-step planning guides and advice for achieving post-high school vocational goals. It can be intimidating for teens to determine what steps they will need to take to realize their career goals while still in high school or immediately after graduation. These books serve as road maps, guiding teens through this time in their lives.

Brian McAllister and Mike Marriner even used the word road map in the title of their book. In *Roadmap: The Get-It-Together Guide for Figuring Out What to Do with Your Life,* they take readers along on their travels around the world as they interview successful people in numerous careers and discover how a fulfilling vocation is developed. For those teens who are going directly into a vocation or are already in one but aren't satisfied, there are two guides we recommend for advice on switching careers: *The Pathfinder: How to Choose* or *Change Your Career for a Lifetime of Satisfaction* and *Success and Careers: The Graphic Guide to Finding the Perfect Job for You.* In *The Pathfinder,* readers can take more than a hundred self-assessments to determine what careers might be best for them based on personality and aptitude. *Careers: The Graphic Guide* is chock full of infographics, information on possible career paths, industry profiles, and more.

If teens need further guidance and advice, we recommend *What Color Is Your Parachute? for Teens: Discover Yourself, Design Your Future, Plan for Your Dream Job* and *Do What You Are: Discover the Perfect Career for You Through the Secrets of Personality Type.* Both titles walk teens through a journey of self-discovery to identify their strengths and talents, and to help young people connect their strengths to fulfilling career options.

Whether a teen needs help visualizing themselves in a career, choosing their next steps post-high school, or instigating a vocational change, these books are sure to engage young people and help them to find success.

> *The Art of Work: A Proven Path to Discovering What You Were Meant to Do,* Jeff Goins (2015)
> *Careers: The Graphic Guide to Finding the Perfect Job for You,* DK.com (2015)
> *Do What You Are: Discover the Perfect Career for You Through the Secrets of Personality Type,* Paul D. Tieger (2014)
> *In Their Shoes: Extraordinary Women Describe Their Amazing Careers,* Deborah Reber (2015)
> *Maker Pro: Essays on Making a Living as a Maker,* John Baichtal (2014)
> *The Pathfinder: How to Choose or Change Your Career for a Lifetime of Satisfaction and Success,* Nicholas Lore (2012)
> *Relish,* Lucy Knisley (2013)
> *Roadmap: The Get-It-Together Guide for Figuring Out What to Do with Your Life,* Brian McAllister, Mike Marriner, and Nathan Gebhart (2015)
> *Sous Chef: 24 Hours on the Line,* Michael Gibney (2015)
> *Undecided: Navigating Life and Learning after High School,* by Genevieve Morgan (2014)
> *What Color Is Your Parachute? for Teens: Discover Yourself, Design Your Future, and Plan for Your Dream Job,* 3rd edition, Carol Christen (2015)

You Majored in What? Designing Your Path from College to Career,
Katherine Brooks (2010)

BOOKS THAT HELP TEENS TO PREPARE FOR VOCATIONAL EXAMS

Your library likely has a number of vocational exam prep books on the shelves (which may be already checked out by young adults eager to achieve high scores on these tests). There is no shortage of exam prep books available for purchase by libraries; therefore, the list of titles below only touches on the surface. We attempted to include at least one title related to popular vocational exams such as the MBLEx, ASVAB, CNA, and CAST. We have also included study guides for the GED, HiSET, and TABE, because some teens you work with may need to take and pass one of these high school equivalent exams before enrolling in a vocational training program.

These preparatory books should be frequently evaluated for currency and weeded when they are no longer up-to-date. Many publishers release new versions each year, even if a test has not undergone any major changes. When a test has been significantly altered in format, length, or content, it is most important that the old books be taken off the shelves and new versions ordered. This means someone in your library needs to have the responsibility of keeping tabs on when these exams are updated. A method for conducting this check can be put in place for your staff. This may entail a quick check every six months or so to see if there have been any changes to the exam.

For many of the vocational exams, there are sample questions available online or through the subscription databases we will cover later in this chapter. If library staff know about exam resources online, they can point patrons in this direction even if the library does not own the current copy of an exam prep guide or if the book is currently checked out by another user. Another way we can assist teens looking to complete vocational exams is by providing them with quiet study rooms, internet access, desks to spread out their study materials, or a location to meet to study with other students. They may also come to us for help registering for the exam.

The preparatory books listed below would be a great resource for teens who are looking to ace these exams. Teens may not want to spend the money to purchase the books when they know they will not need these resources for long. Therefore, being able to access these free of charge at the library would be very appealing.

> *2017 Journeyman Electrician Exam Questions and Study Guide,* Ray Holder (2017)
>
> *ASVAB: Armed Services Vocational Aptitude Battery,* LearningExpress (2017)
>
> *ASVAB Premier 2017-2018 with 6 Practice Tests: Online + Book + Videos,* Kaplan Test Prep (2017)
>
> *Barron's Firefighter Candidate Exams,* 8th ed., James J. Murtagh and Darryl Haefner (2017)
>
> *Barron's Real Estate Licensing Exams (Salesperson, Broker, Appraiser),* 10th edition, Jack P. Friedman and J. Bruce Linderman (2016)
>
> *CAST Test Prep: Study Guide and Practice Questions for the Construction and Skilled Trades Exam,* CAST Exam Prep Team (2015)
>
> *CDL Study Guide Book: Test Preparation and Training Manual for the Commercial Driver's License (CDL) Exam,* Commercial Driver's License Prep Review Team (2014)
>
> *CNA Exam Preparation 2017: 1000 Review Questions for the Nursing Assistant,* Test Key Points Prep Team (2017)
>
> *CNA Study Guide: Exam Preparation Review Book for the Certified Nursing Assistant Exam,* Certified Nursing Assistant Review Team (2017)
>
> *CSCS Study Guide: Exam Prep and Practice Exam Questions for the NSCA Certified Strength and Conditioning Specialist Test,* CSCS Certification Prep Team (2017)
>
> *GED Preparation 2017: Study Guide Book and Test Prep for All Subjects on the GED Exam,* GED Study Guide Test Prep Team (2017)
>
> *HiSET Exam 2017–2018 Strategies, Practice and Review,* Kaplan Test Prep (2017)
>
> *Journeyman Plumber's Exam Secrets Study Guide: Plumber's Test Review for the Journeyman Plumber's Exam,* Plumber's Exam Secrets Test Prep (2013)
>
> *MBLEx Study Guide: Test Prep Book and Practice Exam Questions for the Massage and Bodywork Licensing Examination,* MBLEx Test Prep Review Team (2017)
>
> *Medical Assistant Exam Prep: Practice Test + Proven Strategies (Kaplan Medical Assistant Exam Review),* Kaplan Nursing (2017)

TABE Test Study Guide 2018-2019: Exam Review Book and Practice Test Questions for the Test of Adult Basic Education, TABE Exam Prep Team (2017)

BOOKS TO HELP TEENS FIND THE RIGHT CAREER OR DEGREE/ CERTIFICATE PROGRAM

Recently, we had a conversation with a small group of teens about college preferences. One teen in the group announced that she wanted to go to Duke University. Another teen argued that the University of North Carolina Chapel Hill was just as good or better. The first teen replied, "Maybe. But Duke has the better medical program and I want to be a cardiothoracic surgeon." We were impressed that the teen had such a clearly defined goal and knew how she wanted to go about achieving it. However, this is not always the case. Not all teens know how to go about accomplishing their career goals. When a teen is unsure where to turn, library staff can point them to one of the following books.

The Book of Majors 2018 is a thorough and definitive guide to college majors. In it, the editors list the top 200 college majors in the United States, and which colleges offer them. This guide also lists technical and vocational certificate options. This is the only guide available that shows all this information in one place.

If the teen you are assisting has already decided that nursing is the major for him or her, you can skip the wide-ranging *Book of Majors 2018* and instead point them to *Peterson's Nursing Majors 2017*. While similar in size and scope, this tome focuses just on nursing programs in the United States. Featuring profiles of over 3,900 undergraduate, graduate, and postdoctoral nursing programs, this comprehensive guide is generated with input from the American Association of Colleges of Nursing.

Even if a teen has struggled in high school, college is still very much a viable option. The Princeton Review published *The K & W Guide to Colleges for Students with Learning Differences: 353 Schools with Programs or Services for Students with ADHD, ASD, or Learning Disabilities,* 13th edition. This guide will help students who may have learning challenges plan their journeys to college. There are many colleges that offer programs specifically tailored to different learning styles and the *K & W Guide* is an invaluable resource to teens who may need extra support as they pursue vocational certificates or college degrees.

The College Board Book of Majors 2018, The College Board (2017)

The K & W Guide to Colleges for Students with Learning Differences: 353 Schools with Programs or Services for Students with ADHD, ASD, or Learning Disabilities, 13th Edition, Princeton Review (2016)

Peterson's Nursing Programs 2017, Peterson's (2016)

BOOKS THAT HELP TEENS FIND FUNDING FOR SCHOOL

One of the greatest challenges for some young people who have the desire and drive to pursue a trade is how to secure the funds needed for entry exams and application fees, and later to pay for their coursework, textbooks, needed technology, and even their transportation to and from classes. Unfortunately, this financial challenge can seem unsurmountable, keeping some very bright young people from achieving their fullest potential. Before we started researching trade schools, we didn't even know that financial aid and scholarships were available for students attending these programs. Librarians can help those interested in pursuing trades to locate the needed funding. The books in this section can serve as resources to help you help interested teens consider all the options for funding their education.

Titles such as *How to Graduate Debt-Free: The Best Strategies to Pay for College #NotGoingBroke* and *Paying for College Without Going Broke, 2018 Edition: How to Pay Less for College* will provide insight to help students graduate without carrying with them a huge financial burden.

We have also included books to help students research available scholarship options and to provide techniques for securing these scholarships. *How to Write a Winning Scholarship Essay: 30 Essays That Won Over $3 Million in Scholarships* includes thirty examples of winning essays with analysis; in contrast, the authors include twelve unsuccessful scholarship essays and analyze why they failed. There are many scholarship guidebooks that can help teens locate what's available to them. *The Ultimate Scholarship Book 2019: Billions of Dollars in Scholarships, Grants and Prizes* includes specific information about these sources of funding, including all pertinent information regarding deadlines, qualification requirements, and where to access the applications. *Peterson's Scholarships, Grants and Prizes 2018* is another popular guidebook. Both guides are updated annually to provide the most current information, so be sure to replace these guides as often as your budget will allow. However, even an older version of the guide can be useful to start a search after which you can help teens employ the internet to locate more up-to-date information as needed.

> *Colleges That Pay You Back, 2017 Edition: The 200 Schools That Give You the Best Bang for Your Tuition Buck,* Princeton Review and Robert Franek (2016)
>
> *Confessions of a Scholarship Winner: The Secrets That Helped Me Win $500,000 in Free Money for College— How You Can Too!,* Kristina Ellis (2013)
>
> *How to Graduate Debt-Free: The Best Strategies to Pay for College #Not GoingBroke,* Kristina Ellis (2016)
>
> *How to Write a Winning Scholarship Essay: 30 Essays That Won Over $3 Million in Scholarships,* Gen Tanabe and Kelly Tanabe (2018)
>
> *Paying for College without Going Broke, 2018 Edition: How to Pay Less for College,* Princeton Review, Kalman A. Chany, and Geoff Martz (2017)
>
> *Peterson's Scholarships, Grants and Prizes,* Peterson's (2018)
>
> *Scholarship Handbook 2018,* The College Board (2017)
>
> *The Ultimate Scholarship Book 2019: Billions of Dollars in Scholarships, Grants and Prizes,* Gen S. Tanabe and Kelly Y. Tanabe (2018)

BOOKS TO HELP PARENTS HELP THEIR TEENS

Sometimes library staff are approached by teens accompanied by their parents, who are also looking for advice. From pregnancy through teenagerhood, parents turn to advice books. Now we can hand them books to help guide families through the college admissions process as well.

For parents of teens who are still seeking their vocational calling, we recommend *How to Launch Your Teen's Career in Technology: A Parent's Guide to the T in STEM Education, Originals: How Non-Conformists Move the World,* and *Brainstorm: The Power and Purpose of the Teenage Brain.* These three books can help parents and teens think through unique career options. The authors provide tools to help identify talents and turn them into viable career options. As a bonus, these three titles provide insight into the chemistry and science of the teenage brain.

Two additional titles that speak to the biological development of the teenage brain are *Untangled: Guiding Teenage Girls Through the Seven Transitions into Adulthood* and *Helping Your Anxious Teen: Positive Parenting Strategies to Help Your Teen Beat Anxiety, Stress, and Worry.* These books help parents to understand what makes their teens' brains unique, and how they can work with their children to amplify their strengths while overcoming challenges.

Last but certainly not least, we would like to recommend some titles that provide parents with proven methods to help their teens succeed as adults. The authors of *Smart but Scattered Teens: The "Executive Skills" Program for Helping Teens Reach Their Potential* provide a research-proven program for promoting independence by building executive skills such as organization, focus, and impulse control. *The Gift of Failure: How the Best Parents Learn to Let Go So Their Children Can Succeed* and *How to Raise an Adult: Break Free of the Overparenting Trap and Prepare Your Kid for Success* advise parents to stop micromanaging their teens and learn how to instead gently guide them into adulthood. Once their teens are officially adults, there's *There is Life After College: What Parents and Students Should Know About Navigating School to Prepare for the Jobs of Tomorrow.* Anxious parents who are concerned that their college students may not have concrete after-graduation plans will be reassured by the author's advice for life after the degree.

> *Brainstorm: The Power and Purpose of the Teenage Brain,* Daniel J. Siegel (2014)
>
> *The Gift of Failure: How the Best Parents Learn to Let Go So Their Children Can Succeed,* Jessica Lahey (2016)
>
> *Helping Your Anxious Teen: Positive Parenting Strategies to Help Your Teen Beat Anxiety, Stress, and Worry,* Sheila Achar Josephs (2017)
>
> *How to Launch Your Teen's Career in Technology: A Parent's Guide to the T in STEM Education,* Charles Eaton (2017)
>
> *How to Raise an Adult: Break Free of the Overparenting Trap and Prepare Your Kid for Success,* Julie Lythcott-Haims (2016)
>
> *Originals: How Non-Conformists Move the World,* Adam Grant (2017)
>
> *Smart but Scattered Teens: The "Executive Skills" Program for Helping Teens Reach Their Potential,* Richard Guare, Peg Dawson, and Colin Guare (2012)
>
> *There Is Life After College: What Parents and Students Should Know about Navigating School to Prepare for the Jobs of Tomorrow,* Jeffrey J. Selingo (2017)
>
> *Untangled: Guiding Teenage Girls Through the Seven Transitions into Adulthood,* Lisa Damour (2017)

BOOKS TO PROVIDE INSPIRATION ALONG THE WAY

Selecting a career that's a good fit and the challenges required to attain the necessary education and certifications to pursue this career can sometimes be daunting, even for those individuals who enjoy school. Now consider a teen who struggled through high school and yet has set his or her sights on becoming a veterinary technician. The path to attaining that goal will take perseverance and discipline. Therefore, we thought it might be helpful to recommend a few titles for the young adult who needs a little inspiration to keep pushing through to completion. Librarians can provide encouragement in person, and we can also send teens home with a book to guide them through the tough moments. If you create booklists for workforce development programs you offer, including some of the inspirational titles discussed in this section will be a source of light reading to complement more content-heavy titles.

Most young adults constantly second-guess their actions and decisions, which can lead to lots of negative self-talk. In *How to Like Yourself: A Teen's Guide to Quieting Your Inner Critic and Building Lasting Self-Esteem*, Cheryl Bradshaw provides techniques for overcoming that inner critic and trusting your instincts more. *The Crossroads of Should and Must: Find and Follow Your Passion* is an exploration of Elle Luna's journey as an artist as she learned to trust herself and follow her passion, even when she was frightened about whether she could find success on that path. *Stuff That Sucks: A Teen's Guide to Accepting What You Can't Change and Committing to What You Can* is another book that might help teens move through some of those troublesome moments when they try to determine the next step to take towards selecting a career.

We have included several journals and workbooks in this section. These may not be a good fit for the library shelves because patrons would not be able to write in these books. You may want to order a copy of one of these titles to view some sample questions to ask teens to help them explore their interests and goals. For example, *Start Where You Are: A Journal for Self-Exploration* contains thought-provoking prompts that will lead teens to explore their creativity and interests. These journals could also make terrific giveaways at programs for teens or to raffle off at larger events.

The Anxiety Survival Guide for Teens: CBT Skills to Overcome Fear, Worry, and Panic, Jennifer Shannon and Doug Shannon (2015)

Becoming Me: A Work in Progress: Color, Journal and Brainstorm Your Way to a Creative Life, Andrea Pippins (2016)

Conquer Negative Thinking for Teens: A Workbook to Break the Nine Thought Habits That Are Holding You Back, Mary Karapetian Alvord and Anne McGrath (2017)

The Crossroads of Should and Must: Find and Follow Your Passion, Elle Luna (2015)

Feel Good 101: The Outsiders' Guide to a Happier Life, Emma Blackery (2017)

Good Enough, Paula Yoo (2012)

Hey, It's Okay to Be You, Jessie Paege (2017)

How to Be a Bawse: A Guide to Conquering Life, Lilly Singh (2017)

How to Like Yourself: A Teen's Guide to Quieting Your Inner Critic and Building Lasting Self-Esteem, Cheryl Bradshaw (2016)

Q & A a Day for Me: A 3-Year Journal for Teens, Betsy Franco (2014)

Rising Above: How 11 Athletes Overcame Challenges in Their Youth to Become Stars, Gregory Zuckerman (2017)

Start Where You Are: A Journal for Self-Exploration, Meera Lee Patel (2015)

Wreck This Journal (Duct Tape) expanded edition, Keri Smith (2012)

You Got This! Unleash Your Awesomeness, Find Your Path, and Change Your World, Maya Penn (2016)

ONLINE RESOURCES

In addition to physical books, many libraries now offer their patrons access to online resources. Self-paced instruction helps teens to develop skills necessary for success after high school. Most of the resources require a paid account, but your library may offer free access to patrons with a library card. BrainFuse's HelpNow, Khan Academy, and Tutor.com offer academic assistance such as homework help to students ranging from elementary school through college. HelpNow and Khan Academy feature video tutorials that break down problem-solving techniques into simple, common-sense methods, and Tutor.com has professional tutors to help students with their assignments in real time.

LearningExpress Library would be a terrific tool for students preparing for life after high school. This resource has practice tests for all the most common exams: ACT, SAT, AP, TOEFL, GRE, GMAT, LSAT, MAT, MCAT, GED, HiSET, and TASC. Students can take an assortment of tests as many times as they wish and receive feedback on questions they missed to help them prepare for the real test.

BrainFuse's JobNow is a partner to its HelpNow. This resource can assist library patrons when they've graduated from school and are ready to enter the workforce. Chock full of interactive online help, live interview coaches, resume resources, and personality and aptitude tests, JobNow is a valuable resource for anyone looking for a job.

Whether teens are still in high school or about to enter college, they can benefit from skills taught on Lynda.com. We have recommended this resource to everyone from preteens to adults. It contains thousands of video tutorials that cover hundreds of technological skills.

CONCLUSION

The resources covered in this chapter are meant to serve as a jumping-off point for thinking through the ways your library serves teens and young adults on the brink of entering what will hopefully be lucrative and fulfilling careers. We could not include every available resource in this chapter. However, we hope these titles will serve to inspire you as you think about how your library can best assist the young people in your community. Of course, each collection will differ according to the specific needs of your patrons.

Once you purchase resources like the ones listed in this chapter, be sure to spend some time brainstorming how to best market them. You could bring these titles on visits to schools or camps, compile online or print booklists, highlight reviews of titles on your website or in your library, partner with school guidance counselors, share these titles during programs, or create eye-catching book displays. There are many ways to feature a career-related collection that will catch the attention of teens, teachers, or parents who may find these resources highly valuable.

Note

1. Stephen Horelick, Dennis Neil Kleinman, and Janet Weir, *Reading Rainbow Theme Song*, 1983.

Sample Fast Track: Trade School Fair
Workshop Evaluation

WORKSHOP EVALUATION: Participant

Did you enjoy this career readiness program? Let us know what you thought about today's class, and ideas you have for other sessions.

Library:_____ Session:_____ Date:_____

Name: _____ Age: _____

School: _____

After attending this program I feel more prepared for a career.

☐ I agree   ☐ I disagree

Do you have any suggestions for future library programs? Please let us know:

_____

_____

_____

_____

Thank you for providing feedback about our programs.
Please return this survey to a library staff member.

WORKSHOP EVALUATION: Parent/Guardian

Did you and your teen enjoy this career readiness program? Let us know what you thought about today's class, and ideas you have for other sessions.

Library:_____ Session:_____ Date:_____

Name: _____ Teen's name: _____

After attending this program I feel my teen is more prepared for a career.

☐ I agree ☐ I disagree

Do you have any suggestions for future library programs? Please let us know:

_____

_____

_____

_____

Thank you for providing feedback about our programs.
Please return this survey to a library staff member.

Sample Fast Track: Trade School Fair Flyer

Sample Fast Track: Trade School Fair E-mails

INITIAL INVITATION LETTER (Sent at Least Two Months in Advance)

Good morning,

ImaginOn would like to invite Job Corps to join us again this year for our second annual trade school fair on March 19, 2016, from 2–4 pm. This free event is called "The Fast Track: Trade School Fair" and is for teens and young adults. Last year we welcomed approximately 300 attendees and hope to grow this number this year. I am writing to invite you to join us to highlight what your program has to offer potential students.

Each program/school will be given a table to showcase informational materials. We are also hoping that each table will feature some type of hands-on demonstration or product that will help potential students envision what it might be like to complete their degree in your program/school. There will be no charge for programs/schools to participate in this event.

Please let me know if you have any further questions. I look forward to hearing back from you about whether you will be able to join us for this event.

Thank you very much.

Amy Wyckoff, Loft Manager
Charlotte Mecklenburg Library
ImaginOn

**Follow-Up E-mail to Schools That Have Agreed to Participate
(Sent Shortly after Initial Contact E-mail)**

Good afternoon,

Thank you for signing up to be part of *The Fast Track: Trade School Fair* to be held at ImaginOn on March 19th from 2–4 pm. We are excited that we will have representatives from over 15 schools in the Charlotte area. Please see the attached flyer and additional planning details below.

- Please arrive between 1:00 and 1:30 pm so that you will be all set up by the start of the event at 2 pm.
- Please feel free to bring any material about your school to pass out.
- If you have any hands-on items to bring that will help students to understand what your program is like, please bring these to display on or next to your table.
- If you would like to have a student from your school join you (either currently attending or recently graduated), we think teens and young adults would enjoy the opportunity to ask them questions.
- You will be assigned a standard 7-foot plastic table. There is no need to bring your own. We will also have chairs available.
- You may park in the garage below ImaginOn (entrance on 6th street). We can give you a parking pass when you leave.

Please let me know if you have any additional questions about the event. We look forward to seeing you on March 19th!

Thank you.

Amy Wyckoff, Loft Manager
Charlotte Mecklenburg Library
ImaginOn

Internal E-mail Sent to All Staff

Good afternoon,

I wanted to share some information about an exciting event called *The Fast Track: Trade School Fair* to be held at ImaginOn on March 19th from 2–4 pm. This school fair will highlight trades that do not require a 4-year degree. The fair is open to teens, new adults, and their families. We hope it will be very beneficial to those who attend. We are excited that we will have representatives from over 15 schools in the Charlotte area. There is an active listing for the program on the Library's Calendar of Events.

We would appreciate it if you could display the attached flyer for this event at your branch and mention this program to any teens or new adults who may be interested.

This fair is being jointly planned by The Loft staff and Jimmeka Anderson from the Outreach Department. Please let me, Jimmeka Anderson, or Marie Harris know if you have any additional questions about the event.

Thank you very much.

Amy Wyckoff, Loft Manager
Charlotte Mecklenburg Library
ImaginOn

Internal E-mail Sent to Staff Regarding Volunteers

Hi Teen Staff,

ImaginOn will host the second annual Trade School Fair on Saturday, March 19th from 2–4 pm.

We are looking for additional staff to help out during the hours of 1–5 pm (but feel free to just help for part of this time). This is a wonderful opportunity to contribute to a large-scale event and to learn about local vocational programs for teens and new adults in our community. Last year, we had approximately 300 visitors at this event and hope to grow the number this year.

If you are interested in assisting and have secured your supervisor's approval, please let me know and I can send you additional information.

The program details can be found listed on the Library's Calendar of Events.

Thank you for considering helping out,

Amy Wyckoff, Loft Manager
Charlotte Mecklenburg Library
ImaginOn

E-mail to Library Partners That Work with Teens

Hi Lori,

I am writing to share some information about an exciting event called *The Fast Track: Trade School Fair* to be held at ImaginOn on Saturday, March 19th from 2–4 pm. This school fair, which is open to teens and young adults, will highlight trades that do not require a 4-year degree. We hope it will be very beneficial to those who attend.

This school fair is free to attend. Free raffle tickets will be distributed and include prizes like books, CTC tickets, and earbuds. Groups are welcome to attend. Parents and educators are also invited.

A flyer is attached. We would appreciate it if you could share it with teens and their families.

I look forward to hearing from you.

Thank you.

Amy Wyckoff, Loft Manager
Charlotte Mecklenburg Library
ImaginOn

Thank-You E-mail to Partners/Presenters

Good afternoon,

Thank you so much for being a part of *The Fast Track: Trade School Fair* last weekend! We know the teens and parents who attended had a very engaging and educational experience—we received terrific feedback from those on the way out of the event. Approximately 200 teens, 50 adults, and 20 preteens attended on Saturday.

You can view photos from the fair on the Library's Flickr account.

If you have any feedback or stories to share from your interactions with visitors, I would love to hear from you.

Again, thank you for your participation. We enjoyed partnering with you to make this event happen!

Amy Wyckoff, Loft Manager
Charlotte Mecklenburg Library
ImaginOn

Fast Track: Trade School Fair Planning Document

This is an example planning document that could be used. We included an example from our event in each of the categories below.

Health and Beauty Schools (Nails, Hair, Esthetician, etc.)					
Educational Program	Contact Information	Attending: Yes/No	Contacted By	Notes	Previous Contacts
Carolinas College of Health Sciences	[Contact Name] [Contact Email]	Yes	Victoria	Emailed 1/18; Confirmed via email on 1/19	Previous: [Contact Name] [Contact Email]

Automotive					
Educational Program	Contact Information	Attending: Yes/No	Contacted By	Notes	Previous Contacts
NASCAR Technical Institute	[Contact Name] [Contact Email]	Yes	Victoria	Emailed 1/18; Called [Contact] on 2/8. Possible depending on availability of staff; confirmed 2/9	Previous: [Contact Name] [Contact Email]

Tech/Arts Trades

Educational Program	Contact Information	Attending: Yes/No	Contacted By	Notes	Previous Contacts
Art Institute of Charlotte	[Contact Name] [Contact Email]	No	Victoria	Called on 1/18 and left message. Emailed 1/19	Previous: [Contact Name] [Contact Email]

Culinary

Educational Program	Contact Information	Attending: Yes/No	Contacted By	Notes	Previous Contacts
Community Culinary School of Charlotte	[Contact Name] [Contact Email]	Yes	Paulina	Emailed 1/18	Previous: [Contact Name] [Contact Email]

Communications

Educational Program	Contact Information	Attending: Yes/No	Contacted By	Notes	Previous Contacts
Carolina School of Broadcasting	[Contact Name] [Contact Email]	Yes	Paulina	Emailed 1/18	Previous: [Contact Name] [Contact Email]

Local Community Technical College

Educational Program	Contact Information	Attending: Yes/No	Contacted By	Notes	Previous Contacts
Paramedic— EMS	[Contact Name] [Contact Email]	Yes	Paulina	Website: https://www.cpcc.edu/emstraining/paramedic-training/home-page	Previous: [Contact Name] [Contact Email]

First Responders

Educational Program	Contact Information	Attending: Yes/No	Contacted By	Notes	Previous Contacts
Police Force	[Contact Name] [Contact Email]	Yes	Paulina	Emailed 1/18	Previous: [Contact Name] [Contact Email]

Skill Training

Educational Program	Contact Information	Attending: Yes/No	Contacted By	Notes	Previous Contacts
Iron Yard (Coding/ Programming)	[Contact Name] [Contact Email]	Yes	Victoria	Emailed 1/23	Previous: [Contact Name] [Contact Email]

Funding

Educational Program	Contact Information	Attending: Yes/No	Contacted By	Notes	Previous Contacts
College Foundation NC	[Contact Name] [Contact Email]	Yes	Victoria	Emailed 1/19; called 2/8 and left message	Previous: [Contact Name] [Contact Email]

Time Line

[Date]: Invitation e-mail

[Date]: Planning meeting

[Date]: Follow-up e-mail

[Date]: Finalize list of presenters; Request volunteers

[Date]: Reminder e-mail to participants

[Date]: Distribute flyers to high schools and community organizations

[Date]: Collect supplies, snacks, and giveaways for the event

APPENDIX E

List of State-Based Worker's Resources

Alabama
https://alabamaworks.com

Alaska
www.alaskaworks.org

Arizona
https://arizonaatwork.com

Arkansas
https://www.arjoblink.arkansas.gov

California
www.edd.ca.gov/Jobs_and_Training/Caljobs.htm

Colorado
https://www.colorado.gov/pacific/cdle/workforceresources

Connecticut
https://www.cbia.com/resources/category/workforce-development

Delaware
https://wib.delawareworks.com

Florida
www.floridajobs.org

Georgia
www.georgia.org/competitive-advantages/workforce-division

Hawaii
http://labor.hawaii.gov/wdd

Idaho
https://www.labor.idaho.gov/dnn/idl/JobSeekers.aspx

Illinois
https://www.illinois.gov/dceo/WorkforceDevelopment

Indiana
https://www.in.gov/dwd

Iowa
https://www.iowaworkforcedevelopment.gov

Kansas
https://www.kansasworks.com

Kentucky
https://educationcabinet.ky.gov
https://kcc.ky.gov/Pages/default.aspx

Louisiana
www.laworks.net/WorkforceDev/WFD_MainMenu.asp

Maine
https://www1.maine.gov/labor/workforce_dev/index.html

Maryland
https://www.dllr.state.md.us/employment

Massachusetts
www.mass.gov/massworkforce

Michigan
www.michigan.gov/wda

Minnesota
https://mn.gov/deed/job-seekers

Mississippi
http://mdes.ms.gov

Missouri
https://jobs.mo.gov

Montana
https://montanaworks.gov

Nebraska
https://neworks.nebraska.gov

Nevada
www.nevadaworks.com

New Hampshire
www.nhworks.org

New Jersey
http://careerconnections.nj.gov

New Mexico
https://www.jobs.state.nm.us

New York
https://www.labor.ny.gov/dews-index.shtm

North Carolina
https://www.nccommerce.com/wf

North Dakota
https://www.workforce.nd.gov

Ohio
http://jfs.ohio.gov

Oklahoma
https://oklahomaworks.gov

Oregon
www.worksourceoregon.org

Pennsylvania
www.dli.pa.gov/Businesses/Workforce-Development/Pages/default.aspx

Rhode Island
www.dlt.ri.gov

South Carolina
https://www.scworks.org

South Dakota
http://dlr.sd.gov

Tennessee
https://www.tn.gov/workforce

Texas
www.twc.state.tx.us

Utah
https://jobs.utah.gov

Vermont
http://labor.vermont.gov/workforce-development

Virginia
www.elevatevirginia.org

Washington
www.wtb.wa.gov/WWDS.asp

West Virginia
http://workforcewv.org

Wisconsin
https://dwd.wisconsin.gov

Wyoming
www.wyomingworkforce.org

INDEX

f denotes figures